MOTHERING &
DAUGHTERING

KEEPING YOUR BOND STRONG
THROUGH THE TEEN YEARS

Eliza Reynolds & Sil Reynolds, RN

SOUNDS TRUE
BOULDER, COLORADO

MOTHERING &
DAUGHTERING

DAUGHTERING

Eliza Reynolds

Contents and Keywords

For my dad.
Editor. Friend. Goof-partner-in-crime. Logical rock.
And intrepid reader of first-period stories.

Acknowledgments

To Elizabeth, whose vision and trust in us gave birth to this work. Thank you, Other Mother, for your dry wit and for breaking me open with your written words and your no-nonsense love.

To Carol Donahoe and the Omega Institute, for being crazy enough to trust a sixteen-year-old to teach and for shepherding, cherishing, and promoting our work so wholeheartedly.

To Professor Gail Cohee, for your support and critique, and, above all, for listening—which proved to me that I do indeed have something valid to say.

To Cynthia, for your enthusiasm and expertise, which guided us safely to shore.

To Nan, for carving my voice out of my lengthy monologues, as a master sculptor does a block of stone. You are an artist.

To Haven, for unearthing my vulnerability and meeting my fire with fire. There is some family that we choose.

To Tami, for looking a twenty-one-year-old squarely in the eyes, for providing logical explanations of intuitive phenomena that delight my Capricorn soul, and for being that visionary guide toward even more universal truths.

And to my six anonymous pilot readers, who generously took my rough manuscript into their lives. Their honest and enthusiastic feedback pushed me to reimagine chapter 1.

All the stories in this book are inspired by real people. All names and stories have been altered so that they are unrecognizable, perhaps even to the people themselves. The inspiration and gratitude remain.

To the mothers whose honest journeys showed me how to be able to write this book: Abbey, Anita, Annie, Barbara, Edit, Eileen, Eve, Francie, Felicity, Gina, Gram, Haven, Hilary, Jackie, Jeanne, Judith, Kali, Linda B., Linda K., Livia, Lorraine, Michelle BC, Mimi, Molly, Natalie, Patrice, and Trace.

To the girls who are the heart of this book: Amy, Anna R., Anna T., Annie, Avalon, Becca, Carissa, Corina, Corey, Corrie, Eleni, Elliot, Ella G., Emily, Gen, Gwen, Hannah, Juliet, Kseniya, Laura, Lesheana, Lesley, Liz, Lola, Lucia, Marion (Slade), Melissa, Molly, Moo, Nora, Sascha, Sasha, Sarah, Sophia, and Youbin, and to each and every daughter whose name may have faded but whose energy and heart I will never, ever forget.

To the boys who gave me the sarcasm and strength to follow this to the end and who own my heart more fully then they could ever imagine: Al, Bo, Jami, Jasper, John, Johnny, Jud, Larry, Nick, Odera, Rafi, Reed, Ron, Rueben, Slanch, Tim, and Wiley.

And to my mom, to whom this entire book is an acknowledgment.

A Preface of Sorts

The Promise

THERE IS A BIG CHANCE you didn't choose to be here with my book in your hand. It's much more likely that you're here under mother-pressure-induced circumstances—I get that. Or maybe you *did* choose to be here (I'll be optimistic!), and you picked my book (oh gosh, a mother-daughter book) off the shelf all by yourself! Good job. You get gold stars.

Either way, you're here, right now.

I want to make an agreement with you before you turn the page:

1. I'm going to make you a promise, one teenage girl to another: I vow to be authentic and real, to cut the BS, and to write only from my heart about my true opinions and what I have learned myself.

2. In return, you agree that when you turn the page, you will turn off that judgmental little "what will people think" voice in your head—the one that might say, with as much sassy attitude as physically possible, "Oh, that's not cool," or "Oh, that's so *weird*." I dare you to give something different a chance. Be brave. Be open. No one at school's going to know. You're just reading a book.

A Note

....

THIS BOOK IS TWO BOOKS in one—one for mothers, one for daughters. I'm Eliza, the daughter of this mother-daughter author team, and I wrote this half for you, a teenage daughter. My mom, Sil, wrote the other half for your mom. My mom is actually quite surprisingly cool. We've been working hard on that for a few years now, for example, by asking her to limit the amount of time she breaks out her Motown dance moves in front of my friends (puh-lease, Ma). We wrote one chapter jointly (chapter 7 of the Daughtering side, page 137), and that one is meant for both mothers and daughters to read together *after* having read their own sections. Get it? I hope so, because (speaking from personal experience here) if you don't get it, your mom definitely won't. Have you ever had to explain to your hyperventilating mom where the minimized document went shooting off to? Well, yeah...

Now, go put on your pajama pants and maybe a big hand-me-down tee shirt. Steal someone-bigger-than-you's sweater (I prefer my dad's). Get some chunky socks and leg warmers, and then make a mug of tea (Earl Grey is the best) with whole milk, a big old dollop of honey, and a nice bar of chocolate on the side OR whatever way *you* like to do it. You know what I'm talking about—*get cozy*.

Ready?

Remember our promise?

Now let's do this.

Introduction

HELLO! MY NAME IS ELIZA Alden Reynolds. I am a nineteen-year-old girl (tall, 5'10", with blue eyes and bushy brown hair), and this is my book.

I am *not* a manufactured personality (somebody that somebody else made up). I'm a pretty ordinary, über-gangly, mildly dorky, makeup-adoring teenage girl.

I stagger out of bed *every* morning at 7:30, blink blearily at my red eyes in the mirror, sit down to pee, and almost nod off again. I gossip on the phone—and, darn it, always exceed my mom's phone contract. I read an unhealthy number of fantasy novels, and I dance my butt off for three classes a week until the sweat is literally dripping from my nose and between my boobs and down my back. And I am praising *whoever* is responsible for it being an *all girls* dance class.

I can chow down a chocolate bar in five minutes flat (*if* I'm getting my period the next day), and I make a wicked bowl of macaroni and cheese. I write in my diary when I'm angry, I am take-the-other-guy/girl-out competitive when it comes to sports (in a way that scares me sometimes), but I am absurdly uncomfortable when it comes to fighting *over* guys. AND I just happened to be out-of-my-mind plain insane enough to spend my "prime" teenage years writing a book *with my mom*.

Now why, you might ask, would an apparently sane (and possibly cool) teenage girl EVER write a book with her mom? I can think of *three* reasons:

First, I wrote this book *because it's personal*. I am a hardened survivor, turned "thriver," of the teen years. I have jumped up and down on my bed for the sheer ecstasy of the moment. I have spread myself out on the floor starfish-style, chest heaving, nose-snotting, and asked the ceiling an aching "WHY?" I have bitten pillows in frustration, slammed doors in irrational anger, and compulsively eye-rolled until my mom and dad worried—95 percent sarcasm and 5 percent true concern—that I would lose the balls somewhere in the far reaches of my cranium. I have made my mom cry with the frosty distance I put between us—just to prove that I could, that I was "big enough" to hurt her, too. And it felt *terrible* but at the same time bitterly satisfying.

I wrote this book as a teen girl *for* teen girls (yes, like YOU!), because I believe that I have something worth sharing from my own trip to the other side of the mother-daughter teen "battle-field." So if you like, imagine me here reporting back, heels clicking, and a wobbly hand saluting on my brow, as one of the lucky ones.

I am part of a mother-daughter duo and of an unlikely duet: a dance of bodies, hearts, and messy human minds; of expectations, grudges, and utterly unrealistic hopes, suspended like giant, invisible hot-air balloons just waiting to expire. We are a pair who broke the cycle, who tossed out the mother-daughter inheritance that had been handed down to us, and who built something better—a real, trusting, loving, honest-to-goodness bond.

I also wrote this book *because I am worried about us teenage girls*. First off, we have just about the worst word-on-the-street stereotype. Supposedly we're bossy, we're bitchy, we're selfish, we have no self-confidence, we're shallow, we're mean, and above all, we are emotional terrors. The year I turned thirteen, my mom was asked for the first time, "Oh, you have a teenage girl? I'm so sorry. How's it going?" Like I was something you had to survive—a disease or a particularly bad pet ("Oh gosh, did Eliza get into the trash again?"). I mean, how often do we hear the vindictive refrain quoted to the exhausted parents of a "terrible two-year-old": "Oh, you think this is bad? Just wait until she's a teenager!" Oh, yes, consider yourself warned.

Well, I'm over it, and I think that you may be, too. So that's another reason I wrote this book. I am *over* society's stereotypes of teenage girls. I may be feisty and a little bit sassy, but I am also kind, intelligent, loyal, and loving—and, by the way, the word is *LEADER*, not "bossy" (have you ever heard a boy called *bossy?*). This book is a declaration of who we *are* and who I believe we *can* be.

I wrote this book because I know that mother-daughter relationships are vitally, frighteningly, and perhaps frustratingly *important* in our teen lives. I am writing this to you with absolute urgency because I know without question that (1) having a good relationship with your mom makes teenage life so much easier, and (2) having a fractured, resentful, or unhappy relationship with your mom means you will be fighting her—and the demons your relationship has given you (call it "baggage" or "emotional inheritance")—for the rest of your life.

Look around your circle of friends for firsthand evidence: a healthy, supportive, and loving relationship with your mom tends to produce a healthy, happy, relatively stable, self-reliant young individual. And I propose the revolutionary concept that we, as teenage daughters, can—and *must*—be right in the middle of the process. No relationship works without both people being an active part of it. (Haven't we seen evidence of that in enough marriages and romantic relationships?) And we are fools—and the rest of the world is, too—if we imagine that *our* relationship with our moms can carry on smoothly *without* us being involved. Ladies, it's time to get smart. The relationship we want only comes when we are in fact a part of it.

Finally, I wrote this book *for the girls who want something deeper*, something more real, honest, and, yes, more meaningful than the teen girl world is offering. I wrote this book for my childhood best buds and my "adopted" little sisters, for the hundreds of girls I have taught, and FOR YOU, the girl I imagine cozily curled up reading this book. I wrote this book for the part of these girls and the part of you, the part of us ALL, that wants something REAL. I wrote it for the part of you that gets *pissed off* when people pretend to be something they're not or when you feel you have to say, "Oh, I'm good," when the very absolute *last* thing you are is "good." For the part of you that loves *real* friends and *real* talks. Do you get what I mean? I think you do, because our teenage life is overflowing with people doing the exact opposite.

I believe in the power of teenage girls to be utterly sane and not some kind of emotionally unstable natural disaster and (I'm really not exaggerating here) *to change the world* from the inside out.

Full disclosure: *I find mother-daughter relationships fascinating.* I know, I know, that sounds an *itsy bit* bizarre, so let me give you some personal background. When I was fifteen years old, I began teaching weekend workshops with my mom, Sil, for mothers and their teenage daughters. Based on our relationship (trust me when I say it is far from perfect, but it is pretty darn good), on my mom's professional work in leading workshops (mainly for women on the topic of body image), and on my summers spent as a counselor at an alternative theater camp, we mashed together a weekend designed to help mothers and daughters build a better/stronger/closer/happier/etc. relationship. This book is inspired by our work together.

I was an initial skeptic, I'll admit. A workshop with my *mom?* But something clicked for me that first day when I stood up at the front of the room. I felt that giddy butterfly feeling in my stomach that means excitement; I discovered a real *passion*, something that lights up both my brain *and* my heart. And dang, a gift that arrives on your lap like that can be so rare that I was determined to chase that feeling of purpose, meaning, and, yes, *fun*. I didn't want to let it escape me! So, if you think reading a book with your mom or attending a workshop with your mom is seriously—potentially fatally—uncool, imagine *teaching one* with your mom! I was the coolest kid in high school, let me tell you.

Our workshops, initially at the Omega Institute in Rhinebeck, New York, have been filled-to-capacity-in-two-days successful. Now as much as I would *love* to flatter myself and say it was because of our names or our lovely smiling faces in Omega's catalog, I must face the facts. It happened because mothers are worried about their relationships with their teenage daughters. And, quite honestly, I think you might be pretty darn anxious about your relationship with your mom, too.

So, **let's be real** about it: right now, as you grow away from childhood and toward adulthood, your relationship with your mom is changing, for better or for worse, and more often *for the worse.* Do you talk less? Argue more? Spend more time alone in your room when you're home because your mom is just *so irritating* and some good old Internet surfing is one click away? I know I did, but quite honestly, that was often the *exact opposite* of what I wanted. I *wanted* to be close to my mom, I wanted her to *get me* and not be offended when I wanted to be alone. I loved the moments, however rare, when we giggled together and I could honestly tell her what was on my mind. And here's the thing: I don't think that's just me; I think that might be you, too. In fact, I think that might be *all* of us.

When I was sixteen, I started asking girls in my workshops to define a word that didn't exist in any dictionary I'd seen but that seemed to be missing from our language: *daughtering.* I'd hand out scraps of unlined paper and the bulk pens the workshop center provided and ask the girls: "What if, just like mothering, daughtering was an act we could all do? How would you define *daughtering*?"

Here is my definition:

DEFINE: Daughtering

Being **active** in your relationship with your mom
so that she knows the real you; balancing your independence
with a dependable bond as you grow into your true self

I believed then—and I still believe today—that we teen daughters are trapped in the language of passivity. Although there's no shortage of popular "wisdom" about the many things that mothers should and shouldn't be allowing—*no* yelling, piano practice *every* day after school, and *no* television (or cell phones, or video games, or whatever) until your homework's done—I believe that popular culture has assigned us daughters no role except that of the utterly exasperated and exasperating teen. But you see, *I think there is more to us than that,* and I suspect you think so, too. We have something more to offer than just a passive reaction to or rebellion against our mothers' parenting.

Most teen daughters I know are not *actively* involved in their mother-daughter relationship. Instead they view their role solely as that of the unfortunate recipient of their mom's inept, infuriating, and embarrassing attentions. (Cue, yet again, the eye roll.) Before our moms have even had a chance to adjust to the fact that we're not little kids anymore, we've already given up on them. Worse still, we've inherited the expectation that it will always be this way, that we have no real choice: moms and teenage daughters don't get along, period. As a result, I've found that many girls withdraw from the relationship ("She'll *never* get it, so why try?") instead of admitting that if we do try as the new young adults that we are becoming, then we might just get somewhere. Now there's a concept.

What if your mom were the person you trusted most in the world? And what if she trusted you back? What if she wanted you to just be *you*, without her own agenda and definition of "success"? What if she got you—the *real* you—when you were sad or confused or happy or excited? And what if you, understanding that she is going to make a mess of things sometimes, were able to help *her* get you? What if you gave her feedback every now and then and helped to fix the ruts, fights, and misunderstandings that got in the way—*especially when she just wasn't getting it?*

What if daughters, together, denied the widespread opinion that their moms are their worst enemy during the teenage years? What if daughters could know that their moms are potentially their greatest support as they grow up and become independent? What if your mom was your strongest ally? For some of you, this may seem obvious—your mom and you are already super close. This book will only work to strengthen your bond and keep you tight through the challenges of the teen years to come. For some of you, however, the idea of your mom as your "strongest ally" may seem light years away; it may make you run and duck for cover. Trust me, this book can be your companion on this often-frustrating journey. Either way, what girl wouldn't want a close and REAL relationship with her mom (if it was in reach)? And, let me tell you, daughtering is one of the most important steps in reaching that goal.

The other half of this book is about mothering—hardly a new word, but a rabidly debated concept and practice in our day and age. I want to share my mom's definition of *mothering* with you because (1) I think it is pretty revolutionary, and (2) every now and then our moms may need a reminder of what "mothering" indeed *is:*

DEFINE: Mothering

Raising your daughter to become herself

I love this definition, because although "mothering" is indeed far more complex—as my mom spends a whole half of this book discussing—it boils down to an essential nugget of truth, which you will see reflected in my definition of *daughtering* and without which we are woefully lost. Our "job" as a teenage daughter is to become more and more ourselves, to find the tricky and vital balance of independence and a dependable bond, and to figure out *who* we are and who we want to choose to be outside of our mother's world.

Life as a teenager, as we are told again and again, is about growing into a unique and independent person separate from our mom and our family and our best friends. It's about negotiating that thrilling and often-frustrating middle period between "Mom, I want to hold your hand when you pick me up from school" (come on now, own up, we all remember it) and "Mom, sometimes I just really wish I had my own apartment!" In my opinion, being a teenager means that we are deep in the process of learning to have strength on the inside. It means we are working on how to know what we feel and to trust that knowledge. As daughters, the time that we spend without our mom just being *ourselves*, whatever that means (maybe it's shopping at a certain store, reading a certain book, playing a certain sport), isn't just something that's kind of good to have whenever it works out. It is totally *essential*. It's the time to find out what is at our core. It's independence time. To me, daughtering means tackling our key issues as a teen girl so we can turn around and deal with our relationships with our moms.

This book is also about *that* time, about *you* time, about *girl* time. And in saying that, I don't mean it's all about puberty or sex-ed or how to get a boyfriend (though those are all very important issues, don't get me wrong). It's about being a girl who is growing up and doesn't want to have only a TV Barbie Doll for a role model. In this book, you and I will go from tackling depression, passing sadness, and daily overwhelm to figuring out how we can be our own best friend (having a diary and deeply contemplating the crack in the ceiling are two starting clues!). We will look at the awkward, mysterious, and quite thrilling fact of first periods and becoming "a woman" and the baggage (and gifts) that come with being the next in the never-ending story of your family. We will go to town with emotional tantrums, triggers, teenage roller coasters, and things that piss you off for no reason (like Crocs sandals, people picking their teeth in public, and your mom). We will ask *crucial* life questions (and giggle just a smidge) about love, lust, and losing your mind (among other things). We will dive into body talk: the boobs we may have and the butt we may not have (and how to cope), how *fat* became a dirty word, and a few fresh ways to *stop obsessing* and to start using our brain for something more important than the size of our lovely love handles. We will then take a walk in the park and talk about friendship, how we *know* we can trust some-one, and the *essential* basics of "talking it out," like a REAL (wo)man. And we will tackle daughtering head on. I promise to tell stories upon stories: stories of heroines — some real world, some legendary; stories of real girls in love, lost, losing it, and finding it, or simply questioning it all.

Although this is a book for teenage daughters, I want to take a moment to welcome all readers, of all ages and genders and family roles, to browse their way through my chapters. I write *as* a teenage daughter *for* teenage daughters, but certainly sto-ries of interest and lessons of larger applicability are contained within these pages. It goes without saying that this is not a book explicitly for teenage sons, nor is it a book for the dads of teenage daughters (though I have a fantastic dad myself). It is too huge a feat to hope to contain the entire family in one girl's book. Instead, I have focused my energies on what I consider the most intense, and often most tension-filled, yet potentially most deeply loving relationship of a girl's life — her bond with her mom.

I am an only child and I have written this book from this per-spective. The fact is, no matter how attention-needing your little brother is or how loud your older sister may be, your relationship with your mom *is* unique. And this book is about what happens when you commit to the time this relationship needs, outside of all other family relationships.

As a girl en route to my society's version of "womanhood" (and my genes' version as well), my inevitable road map is my mom, whether or not I choose to follow her footsteps. More often than not, I will spend a large portion of my journey lugging around her unwanted "baggage" (though it may be invisible to my own eye at times). I wrote this book because I believe with all my heart that our bond with our mothers can be strengthened—like a muscle—if we give it the attention it deserves. This vital relationship *must* be examined, not simply ignored, dismissed, or cursed out, in order for us to move forward into the full experience of our own lives. We must learn to *daughter* our mothers! I believe it's terribly and totally *urgent*.

In many ways, this book is the workshop I've always wanted to teach. It's how I've wanted to talk to the girls who come to our Mothering & Daughtering weekends. But then, when twenty-five of them enter the room and bring their twenty-five different attitudes and levels of self-consciousness with them, it's close to impossible to get as personal, honest, and open with each girl as I would like to. But in this book, it's only you and me.

So I'm asking that when you turn the page, you agree to be okay with something that might seem a little dorky (at first) or that you might not want to broadcast around your entire school. Let's for now be okay with reading about and thinking about and talking about you and your mom. After all, no one's going to know. You can read a chapter or two and then put the book on her bedside table. Then she reads and puts it back on yours. If you make this teeny, tiny effort to connect with her (and maybe it's not so big of an effort for you), she'll have to *struggle* to contain her excitement, I promise. Take a deep breath and let her enjoy it, because, bottom line, it will make your life a whole lot easier if you can find a way to get along.

Here are three guidelines to keep in mind as you read this book:

1. **Be real.** In the quiet world of this book, let's cut the fakeness—even, and especially, with yourself, but also as you begin to interact with your mom. I challenge you to be 100 percent genuine and honest about what you feel.

2. **Be kind.** This is one of the greatest challenges in life. Be kind to yourself, your mom, and others.

3. **Be open.** Be open to new ideas, to a mother-daughter book, and to pushing yourself to grow.

Consider keeping a private companion journal as you read this book. Create a space for expression, rejection, exasperation, doodles, and life-changing thoughts. I will mention this journal of yours throughout the book.

Now, my name is Eliza and I ask you to take me as your guide—a mentor, a big sister, or a friend. I am just another teenage girl trying to figure it all out. I promise.

You ready? Let's do this.

1

The Doll in Your Pocket

To be human is to be lost in the woods. None of us arrive here with clear directions on how to get from point A to point B without stumbling into the forest of confusion or catastrophe or wrongdoing. Although they are dark and dangerous, it is in the woods that we discover our strengths.

—ELIZABETH LESSER
Broken Open

ARE YOU AFRAID?

I know that I am sometimes. There are moments when I have been so afraid of life beginning—like becoming-a-grown-up beginning—because then I might discover that I'm a failure, or a total disappointment, or maybe (whispers an especially dark part of my brain) never truly, fully lovable, except by my parents (and they *have* to love me). When I was about thirteen or fourteen, something began to creep up on me—like an itch on my back that I couldn't quite scratch—and my parents started to *drive me crazy* (plain bonkers, red in the face with frustration, irrationally ticked off, justifiably loony, and the like). Frankly, most of the time it was for dumb reasons ("MOM, do you have to move the pans so *loudly*??")

or for reasons I just couldn't understand ("DAD, I don't want you to ask me about my day. No, I just don't feel like talking about it!"). My reactions to them, and the way I began to judge them through every millisecond of every day, were new. And I found that after the first flush of anger or frustration passed (and I huffed out of the room or screamed in the confines of my bedroom closet), it scared me. These new changes made me feel, well, *lonely.*

It began to dawn on me that my parents weren't the perfect people I had imagined them to be. I wondered: If they weren't always consistent and on top of it, then what *is* consistent—always steady and reliable—in life? And if my life is beginning, like I-am-not-a-little-kid-anymore beginning, like in-a-few-years-I-will-likely-be-leaving-home beginning, then *what* and *who* can I depend on? What won't change? What is safe?

And the hugeness of these thoughts near-about burst my head and my heart open.

In this chapter, I want to talk about change—both the scary kinds of change and the exciting kinds (it's usually a little bit of both). And I want to talk about HOW (for goodness, sake!) we can learn to ride the wave of teenage overwhelm and still fall asleep each day with our sanity (mostly) intact. Because I believe that in order to *daughter* well, we have to first invest in ourselves; we have to passionately commit to the process of understanding our inner workings. Then we can give real energy to our relationship with our mom and to know what we *really* want out of it. Therefore, the goal of this chapter is to begin to find our authentic self—the REAL us—beneath the smiles and the crossed arms, beneath the mom's agendas and the dad's expectations (or whoever seems to be setting either of those in our family structure). Once we've found *our* real voice, we can begin to listen to it. And, let me tell you, all else will follow.

Now, if you met me, walked up to me, and shook my hand for the first time (or even hugged me for the hundredth time), you couldn't tell on the outside that I was afraid. No, you'd still see a tall, cheery nineteen-year-old, with hair twice the size of her head and feet that defy semicoordinated brain commands. But I'm telling you now what's on the inside: the fears that line the innermost layer of my thoughts, my heart, and maybe even, if you believe in such things, my soul. These are the fears that aren't *cute* enough to whisper under the blankets at a sleepover. I'm not always afraid, but sometimes—often first thing in the morning, before I've seen anyone's face, and the alarm is buzzing me into a new day—I feel empty, alone, like the bed is a bit too big, and yes, I feel somewhat overwhelmed by it all. Nah, I'm not an emotional train wreck or a "basket case" either; I'm just being brutally honest. I know you'll get it, because here's the secret that I think we all know: *I think, deep down, we are all afraid.*

I don't mean we are afraid all the time—not every moment. But sometimes in bed at night alone, or staring dismally at another English test, or looking around the dinner table, or scanning Facebook late at night, you and I are afraid. And I don't think it's a light passing fear, like that anxiety you get when you pass by that certain dodgy street in town. No, it is a deep question that seems to echo in our very soul, in the very heart of our bodies. And I know I don't have the answers to the questions that keep bubbling up inside, and you may not either (most people don't). Questions like these:

- Who *am* I?
- What am I going to make of my life?
- What happens when I die?
- What is the *meaning* of life? Why am I here, literally, on this earth? Do I matter any more than that ant on the hot pavement?
- What is love? Does marriage mean you love each other forever? Do I have a soul mate?
- Why is my mom the way she is?
- Does God exist? Or "goddess"? Or any kind of higher power?
- What do others think of me? Is this important? Why?

- What will make me happy? Is happiness the most important thing? What *is* the most important thing in this life?

One thing that I have learned, in the few years that I am ahead of you on the teenage track toward "adulthood," is that we humans often hide the truth. We are sent the "adult" message that we *can't* admit to being afraid or overwhelmed or insecure. Gosh, they might look at us funny (or so we are taught) if we admit that we are wondering about some of life's deepest questions. So instead we smile (I know I did) or we shut down something inside of us (I did that, too); we cross our arms; we close the door—all of this seems simpler, easier, and certainly less painful than admitting the hugeness of what we're feeling. And we certainly don't want to *cry* about it (I certainly didn't want to cry about it), because that would mean feeling like we don't have it "all together," or are less than "perfect," or admitting to "losing it"—and I know that I am afraid that most people just won't know what to do when I "lose it."

So instead of talking about the changes that are going on in our inner (and outer) lives, about the big questions, and about the fears, we often leave the room (literally and metaphorically), we leave the relationship ("Mom, stop it, I'm fine!"), we stop cuddling, we stop voluntarily offering out details of our life, we play the "perfect" girl so no one will get worried. And we start to blame others (our moms are often at the top of the list) for *not understanding.* It happens for all of us, with different levels of intensity and different methods of separation (maybe it's once in a blue moon that you storm into your room or maybe it's three times a day). My dear reader, we are growing up. We are becoming an independent self, which is far bigger, far scarier, and far more *exciting* than seven-year-old me ever could have imagined.

I have spent a lot of my time being excited about "growing up." I think about things like dream jobs, cool places to visit, wedding gowns (yeah, I'll fess up, I've clocked a number of hours debating sleeve preferences to myself), living with my friends instead of my parents, and, in general, just the supreme awesomeness of, one hazy day in the future, having it all "figured out." And although I think that this last bit might be an illusion (no one really does have it as "figured out" as we'd like to think), I admit that I dream of being in control of my life and being able to choose for myself the next mountain I want to climb. Because that's what "big kids" do. But I also think that all too often, the other side—the dark, the sad, the reflective, or the confused side—goes unacknowledged. We just get on with "figuring it all out," forgetting the big truth that we all know: that we are all—teenagers, adults, even grand-parents—in fact, afraid.

For centuries, philosophers, writers, and religious thinkers have called a time of human change, inner questioning, and even sad-ness, overwhelm, pain, and fear, a "dark night of the soul." This time was, and still is, seen as a necessary and utterly *expected* period when the emotional life of the average person cycles down, and things just plain *aren't that good* for a while. We will, all of us, have many "dark nights" in our lives—those moments, weeks, or months when we feel utterly lost and afraid in the change, chaos, or darkness that seems to be all around. Perhaps you have lived through a dark night already or feel locked in the middle of one now, or perhaps you have never yet been sent head over heels tumbling down the rabbit hole. Either way, do you know what the good thing about a "dark night" is? It is always, *always* followed by the sun rising the next morning and another day.

I particularly like the idea of a "dark night of the soul" because it helps me see my lonely or scared or overwhelmed feelings as *mean-ingful*. They are there for a reason: these questions, fears, obsessions, frustrations, and the oh-so-human pain all help me to grow.

Now I want to tell you a story. I want you to meet Vasilisa, one of the most famous heroines from Russian fairy tales and a teen-age girl with a heck of a dark night to overcome. In many ways, metaphorically speaking, her story is my story—and perhaps her story is your story, too.[1] I have written my version—and OUR version—here, for you. So, for just a sec (or maybe a while longer), unlock that "cool" part of your brain and enjoy a story—just that, a simple, fun, and, yes, *meaningful* story.

The Story of Vasilisa

Once there was a girl named Vasilisa who lived happily with her father and mother in a small cottage in a small village in the northern mountains of Russia. Within their day-to-day lives, everything was as it should be, and the little girl—with auburn hair and hazel eyes, dressed all in blue—did not know of suffering beyond her doorstep. She was not yet old enough to see the suffering of the everyday humans who gathered around their hearths each night at the end of a hard day's work. Vasilisa's life was a small world, made vast by her imagination, within which she had the power to fly into the far-reaching treetops, scurry along the forest floor like a fox, and, yes indeed, plop down in the chairs of Russian royalty, a crown fashioned from the nearest branch of pine upon her brow.

One day, Vasilisa's mother became deathly ill. As she lay dying, she called her young daughter to her and placed in her open hands a little doll that she had made with auburn hair and hazel eyes, dressed all in blue—just like Vasilisa. She instructed Vasilisa to always feed the doll and to keep her safe in the front pocket of her dress.

"This is my blessing to you, dear daughter. Take care of her, and make sure to listen carefully, for she will guide you." And then the mother died.

Yes, she died. One moment she was a breathing, warm, hugging mother body, and the next moment she was gone.

Vasilisa took to sleeping in her mother's castaway dresses, many sizes too large, and she avoided the garden patch of fresh earth that had been so freshly tilled for her mother's spring plantings. But life continues, even when we would will it to halt in its tracks. Soon after, Vasilisa's father found new love again.

Vasilisa's father remarried a widow with two daughters near Vasilisa's age. He thought he had done well for them all, and he congratulated himself that his child would have a mother again. But behind his back, the woman and her daughters tormented Vasilisa. Around the family hearth at night, as Vasilisa sat by her father's feet, the women only dared to make the subtle comments that his good heart would allow: "Oh, Vasilisa, your hair is always such a mess—how *special* you look—you've always been a bit of boy, haven't you?" asked her stepmother, and her father chuckled appreciatively and patted Vasilisa on the head. "Oh, Vasilisa, are you going to wear *that*?" "Oh, Vasilisa, I can't believe you said *that*?" her stepsisters cackled. They hated Vasilisa because they were jealous of her beauty, which was on the inside and out. She was patient, kind, and hardworking. She had good sense and good humor, and she believed in the inherent goodness of each living creature.

It wasn't long before the three women had enough of Vasilisa's kind ways and began to plot against her. The stepmother devised an evil plan: They would let the fire in their hearth go out, and complaining of the cold, they would send Vasilisa into the dark woods to beg for fire from the witch Baba Yaga. They knew that Baba Yaga, a fearsomely ugly and terrible creature, half-beast and half-hag, would kill her and eat her! And then they would be rid of Vasilisa forever.

Baba Yaga means "Grandmother" in Russian, and she was thus named in reference to her tremendous age. Baba Yaga lived in the heart of the woods that began at the edge of the village. She had no partner and, to the best of everyone's knowledge, no children to speak of. Instead, she had adopted seven mangy cats. The few teenagers who wandered into her clearing—mostly youths eager to test their young adult "bravery"—returned with tales of ghosts, witchcraft, and a crotchety old woman with thick and matted white hair that fell below her knees; breasts that hung unsupported like the thin udders of an old cow; and a little beard that curled its way in white tendrils along her chin. Word had it that she sat on her rocking chair at the top of her porch steps shrieking obscenities at anyone and anything that crossed her path.

Unsuspecting of her stepmother's trickery and eager to help, Vasilisa set out that very evening on the dark, winding path into the woods. She was frightened and soon became lost, for she had never been into the woods before. She took comfort, however, in the small doll her mother had given her, pressing her palm against the warm spot in her front pocket. In the woods, the branches were so thick that no moonlight made it onto the path below, and no matter how hard she squinted, Vasilisa could not see her feet. In the depths of a despair that she felt certain would swallow her up, she curled up at the base of a great pine tree and fell asleep, with her doll tucked protectively into the curve of her belly.

In the morning, when she woke and looked around her in the gloom of the scarce dawn light, she felt a hollowness in her stomach and a heaviness in her heart, for she was alone. But then she again remembered the little doll with auburn hair and hazel eyes that her mother had given her. Cradling it in her palm, she fed it bread and water, and both felt replenished. Tucking the doll into her front pocket, Vasilisa scrambled to her feet and continued her journey. As she went on, she found that at each fork in the road, the doll miraculously seemed to speak, showing her which path to take. Vasilisa trusted the doll's strong little voice and continued bravely onward.

Finally Vasilisa came to the fearsome hut of Baba Yaga. Even she had to admit it was in a beautiful spot—set around by great tall trees and wildflowers growing up between the cracks of her front steps. But its beauty ended as nature had intended it: the house itself was a wreck. The walls of the little hovel were dank and dripping with leaks from its sagging roof, and Vasilisa was quite sure she spied the beady eyes of a rat peeking out from the darkness of the doorframe behind the witch's feet. Trembling from chilly fingers to chilly toes, Vasilisa looked upon Baba Yaga for the first time.

"What do you want, girl?" demanded the old witch, peering down at her.

"Grandmother . . . " said Vasilisa, feeling her mouth go dry.

"SPEAK UP!" Baba Yaga shrieked.

"I come for fire, Grandmother. My family's hearth has gone cold," replied Vasilisa.

"Well, well, well. I will give you the fire, you good-for-nothing child, but only—ONLY—if you are able to complete all of the tasks I ask of you. Should you fail, well then I will kill you and eat you!" The girl felt herself shrink away from such a terrible possibility, but the doll her mother had given her whispered from her pocket and assured Vasilisa that all would be well.

Vasilisa set to work immediately, but the tasks that were demanded of her were impossible: sorting tiny poppy seeds out of a pile of dirt, finding a needle in a haystack, and the like. That first night in the witch's hovel, as Baba Yaga slept, Vasilisa broke down in tears and gave all up for lost in the face of such overwhelming tasks. But the doll in her pocket spoke to her and told her to feed them both a little and to sleep. In the morning when she woke, the doll had completed the tasks for her! It came to be that however crabby the old witch was, as she stomped around the crumbling hovel in a foul mood, Vasilisa found her way through each day with the doll in her pocket—cooking the crone's breakfast and sweeping the floors clean of rat droppings with good cheer.

After three months of such work, with the doll as Vasilisa's faithful guide, Baba Yaga at last called the young girl to her and, crankily thanking her, released Vasilisa from her service.

"You are a mystery to me, GIRL, but you may have the fire you came a-begging for. Treat it with respect, for it is both precious and powerful."

The witch then reached into her hearth fire and pulled out a blazing branch, which she offered to Vasilisa. The girl hesitated, afraid that the fire would burn her hands.

"TAKE IT!" insisted Baba Yaga, "What, are you SCARED, girl?" And the doll in Vasilisa's pocket spoke to her and assured her that the fire could do no harm. Vasilisa reached out and grasped the blazing branch in her two hands.

Vasilisa returned home through the dark woods, her path lit by Baba Yaga's hearth fire, again guided by the faithful instructions of the doll in her pocket. She burst through the front door of her family's home and lit the hearth once more. Her stepmother and stepsisters were shocked, for they had thought that Vasilisa's long absence meant she was dead—and good riddance! The blazing torch, however, acted of its own will and rose up, chasing the evil stepmother and stepsisters out of the house and down the road . . . never to be seen or heard from again.

DEFINE: Metaphor

A thing regarded as symbolic of something else; a figure of speech that uses one object or idea in the place of another, or a comparison that serves as the key to understanding the truth of an idea, object, or feeling
FOR EXAMPLE: "Carrie can be such a mother bear sometimes"
OR: "Sebas was drowning in homework"

Throughout this book I will be pulling out big words like "metaphor" and defining them—words that I think are specifically relevant, generally important, and just all-around illuminating. My definitions are bridges between the worlds of adult dictionaries and teen speak; I want to write the way *we* would actually use a word. For the purposes of citation (because it's always important to trace the route of where our information has come from), let me say that in most cases, I've popped open the nearest search engine and pulled out a few of the choice words and turns of phrase that sound and feel right to me. These sources include merriam-webster.com, dictionary.com, and my trusty old pal the Google search engine. These sources are my inspiration; then my own imagination and experience take hold, and what I consider the "real" definition is born. So, the word above, the first word to be defined from the outside world (and not from the internal world of Daughtering), is an example of this defining process of mine: *metaphor*. Why is this word important? And how can you use it in your day-to-day life?

I think that stories are incredibly powerful things. What's the latest book you read or movie you watched that took over your imagination? You know—that story that seemed, for some crazy reason, to really *matter* and to have a meaning and a reality that extended beyond the pages or the screen? What was the last story that made you, sitting on your couch in your pj's, *feel* something (giddiness, melancholy, or even bawling-your-eyes-out sorrow)? Now, if you have ever studied the Greek myths in school or heard the biblical story of Noah's Ark or understood the lasting popularity of a play written hundreds of years ago, such as Shakespeare's *Romeo and Juliet*, then you know the fundamental truth: we humans *crave* stories. We always have. They are our explanations, our inspirations, our warnings, and the entertainment that whisks us out of our humdrum lives. The story of Vasilisa is no different. However, instead of simple amusement, I want to approach the story as a *tool*. I believe stories can be useful. Through the use of *metaphor*, stories can help us make sense of our most authentic, REAL selves.

When you think about it, stories are not always about people outside of us. In fact, many would argue that they are about what is inside of us: the voices and parts of ourselves that live a daily story. You know the evil stepsister who "lives" inside you, right? The one who looked over your shoulder into the mirror this morning and added some "constructive" advice about your outfit or the state of your pimples? For me, she's this specific voice in my head that tends to be rather insecure, superficial, and cruel. When I'm having a bad day, I often feel like I can't shut off her endless babbling critique! In a certain sense, this is the use of *metaphor*: I do not have a literal "stepsister" living in my brain, but sometimes it is like she just popped out of Vasilisa's fairy tale and is hanging around in my head to torture me.

And what about Baba Yaga? This witch is a traditional character from Russian folklore—sometimes she is a cruel, scary old hag, and sometimes, if we are brave enough to ask, she can become a wise old crone or a grandmother, ready to give the truest advice we have ever heard. Baba Yaga does not make life easy for us, but she knows (as we sometimes do not know for ourselves) that pain and hard times can lead to strength and joyous times. She tests us. She is ugly because that scares us, and she lives alone because that is our worst fear. Just as we can have an "evil stepsister" inside of us (or outside of us, roaming the halls of middle school), we can also have an inner Baba Yaga—an eternally wise, perhaps a little crotchety, nonmaterialistic, and brutally honest voice that switches on in the toughest of situations. We may have even met people like her—perhaps a teacher, grandparent, or mentor—in the outside world of our daily lives. Marion Woodman, a wise woman, psychologist, and epic writer on myths and fairy tales, sees Baba Yaga as the ultimate test of growing up: "Sooner or later, we meet Baba Yaga, and how we deal with her will determine whether we remain frightened children or mature into adults."[2] Have you had a Baba Yaga moment?

The story of Vasilisa is a sad one. In fact, it is deeply tragic: in the first years of Vasilisa's life, her mother dies, and her father unconsciously deserts her to the torture of this trio of cruel women. When we "use" Vasilisa's story by laying her life over our own, just as a dressmaker lays a pattern over fresh cloth, we do not "need" to have lost our mom in order to understand Vasilisa's feelings. In a certain way, we have lost a version of our mom by growing up; we have lost a certain type of relationship with her, and a certain view of her, that will never, *ever* come back. And I, for one, feel that this was a quiet, unannounced tragedy of my early teen years. My childhood relationship with my mom had "died," and I realized that I would never be able to 100 percent rely on her as I had before, and that she would never have the answer for my every question again—and nor, perhaps, would I want her to. What a painful human tragedy! I think that the death of Vasilisa's mother, as well as Vasilisa's own ability to move forward by trusting the doll that her mother had given her, is a blueprint for my (and your) teenage lives.

Using the language of metaphor, there are parts of the teenage years that can be like the darkest woods, with not much moonlight seeping through the thick branches of the trees above. I think that the questions we ask or the fears we carry inside are all dark paths in the woods, dark paths inside ourselves, or a dark night of the soul. Elizabeth Lesser is one of my "other mothers" and a personal Baba Yaga of sorts who has pushed me to greater clarity and into darker, more honest places in myself. She writes in her beautiful book *Broken Open: How Difficult Times Can Help Us Grow*, that "to be human is to be lost in the woods." Thus I am lost, and you are lost, and we are all lost! There is no shame in the darkness (or in not smiling *all the time,* as I have been told that "nice" girls do). In fact, it is those of us who do *not* travel into the dark woods—where "we discover our strengths," where our doll guides us, and Baba Yaga's fire lights our path home—that I am most concerned about.

Vasilisa's story is also an answer to our huge, teenage questions: How do we deal with the tough times and changes that may be painful (and perhaps positive at the same time)? How do we deal with dark woods? How do we deal with questions so impossible to answer that we feel as if they may swallow us whole? I think that the answer is right there in the story, in Vasilisa's front pocket: the doll. Vasilisa's doll is a voice "within" her that only she can hear. It is a sensible presence that guides her through the dark paths and that seems to know the way almost instinctually. Elizabeth Lesser believes that although we may feel lost, we are never truly alone — for an inner guide can lead us. At the close of her book, *Broken Open,* she writes this wish for all of us: "If you are lost, may you understand that we are all lost, and still we are guided . . . by the vibrant voice within the beat [of our heart]. May you follow that voice, for *this is the way* — the hero's journey, the life worth living, the reason we are here." For me, that vibrant voice within is the doll in my pocket.[3]

Do you have a little voice like this? That voice that seems to come from your gut or your heart and shout out at you in the middle of a difficult situation? I would say that Vasilisa's doll is a metaphor for what some call "intuition." Have you ever heard of this word? Here is my definition:

DEFINE: Intuition

That little voice inside of you that knows what to do, that knows what's really up; that gut feeling you have about a person or a situation; from the Latin *intueri,* which is often roughly translated as "to gaze at" or "to contemplate"

Intuition is a simple and crucial tool for all teens to have in their pocket. In fact, I believe that intuition, or self-trust, is *the* antidote for teen overwhelm and angst, and it is one of the keys to our future joy and contentment in life as adults. I think that learning how to trust yourself when you just *know* something, even if that knowing isn't rational or logical in the slightest, is going to make the next few years (and the rest of your life) *so* much easier. Our intuitive voice (the voice of the doll in our pocket) is the voice of our most authentic self trying to get our attention. You know the kind of knowing I'm talking about, right? And I think you know the trouble you can get into when you don't pay attention to it.

Let's take an early example from my life: When I was in fifth grade, I had this huge problem listening to that little voice in my head that told me *not* to share my secrets with any popular girls who happened to smile at me and act like we were friends. This included the time I told Selena about my crush. I desperately wanted to be a cool, older girl who liked a boy (yes, the priorities of my fifth-grade self). But then Selena went and told him. Ouch. But I also do absolutely remember this emptied-out feeling in my stomach as I whispered into Selena's cupped ear, "I like Rob. Don't tell." Even as the words leaked from my mouth, I knew that I should have kept my secret to myself. This wasn't a logical knowing (Selena did promise not to tell). I just *knew*.

I am trusting my gut (yes, my *intuition*) when I don't get in the car of the kid I don't know all that well. When I feel that twist in my stomach, I smile and pretend to pick up the phone, making any old excuse I need for staying behind ("Gosh, my mom is, like, so annoying, but she's making me stay home tonight"). And maybe sometime in the future, I'll learn to tell the complete truth: "Sorry, y'all. I'm just not that comfortable with this."

No matter your age, having confidence in what you yourself feel, know, and believe is essential. Intuition has been a guiding light when I am feeling the darkest, because knowing and acting on what I feel is right—on what I feel I truly *need*—will always set me straight. We can be friends with ourselves. We can comfort ourselves when we're afraid, because we *know* what makes us feel comfortable again. We can calm ourselves down when we're angry. And when faced with an especially difficult situation, we can reason things out with a pen and paper or in a full conversation with our bedroom walls—as I *may* have been known to do.

Imagine a doll in your pocket, like the one Vasilisa had, but one that looks like you. What does she look like? Actually visualize her for a moment. What color is her hair? And her eyes? Is she sporting ripped jeans or maybe a summer dress? A ponytail or two spunky braids? You can carry your intuition in your pocket. With that priceless friend, you are never alone, because you always have yourself to trust. *Dorky?* Maybe. *True?* Utterly.

Intuition Guidelines

So, how can we learn to hear, value, and actually follow our gut? How can we use our intuition (this whole big concept) in everyday life? The voice of our intuition is *smart*—like, really smart—if we could only learn to listen. There is more than one type of intelligence (as I will discuss in chapter 3). We can get all out of balance if we listen only to the one kind of intelligence that is the most valued in our culture: the logical and the academic intelligence that, for example, we're tested on each day in school. Instead, we have to tune our ability to hear our intuition; we have to train our ear to find our intuition's voice. And here, I think, is how we can do that:

1. I recommend that you start learning to listen to your gut: that anxious feeling in your stomach, that tension in your shoulders, that antsiness in your feet. If you start to heed that unpindownable sense of worry, which may just be a nagging (but incomplete) "But . . ." in your brain, then you will find the key to a different kind of "smart" inside you. *You have to train yourself to pay attention.* Really pay attention. This "other knowing" contains valuable information, and the sooner you start to listen to it, the easier your life will be. Open up your "intuition ears."

2. If you don't understand what your intuition (whether it's a physical sensation or a sense of worry) is trying to tell you, or if you are not sure if you can hear it, try this:

a. **Talk it out.** Talk about it with someone who *gets* you and won't put his or her own agenda on the situation. Talk with someone you can be 100 percent honest with and not feel embarrassed. Believe it or not, this might be an adult, though not necessarily your parents. The wisdom of experience shouldn't be discounted.

b. **Write it out.** Write out what you *think* your intuition may be telling you, even if you don't know for sure. In a journal, on a loose piece of printer paper, on whatever's nearby . . . just write out the first thing that comes to your head. Don't put your pen down until you've figured it out. Be 100 percent honest with yourself, even (and especially) if you feel guilty or ashamed about the way you feel.

c. **Think it out.** Lie down in bed, or on the couch, or outside under a tree. Look up. Give yourself at least fifteen minutes to just think out every twist and turn of the situation and to think about the feeling you're having in your gut. You don't have to come up with any solutions right now.

d. **Sleep on it.** Give yourself the time to pause and reflect on it during a good night's sleep, just as Vasilisa's doll told her to do. Sometimes intuition can be confused with fear and we can act impulsively. Giving myself an extra day to think it through often turns my conclusion to clarity. Intuition comes into this clarity and a feeling of certainty results.

3. Go with your gut. After listening to and understanding this "other knowing," we then have the choice of how to act. Often that means doing something difficult: standing up for someone or something you believe in, apologizing when you know you made a mistake, saying *no* to something you *know* you don't want or just aren't ready for. It's one thing to understand what

your intuition is telling you, and it is another, sometimes harder, thing to act on it. Actually, I think that following your gut is just another way of saying that you are being true to yourself.

If we begin to live according to our intuition, then we can begin to live our life as our most REAL self—genuine, honest, heartfelt, and so on. And I don't know about you, but I for one think my *real* self is my best and happiest self. What better thing to strive for?

Life and dark nights (of the "soul" or lost in the "woods") are rarely simple. They are more often like an emotional roller coaster. I feel excited *and* scared at the same time! I feel pissed off *and* kind of relieved! I feel destroyed *and* oddly calm. Intuition is a kind of smart that helps us understand these apparent contradictions, or paradoxes, in life. *Paradox* is one of my favorite words, because it fits the reality of my teen life.

DEFINE: Paradox

A person, thing, or situation that seems contradictory, impossible, or absurd but that in reality expresses a possible truth

---

What is a paradox? It is the bittersweet feeling you get when two apparently contradictory things can and *do* exist at once. Have you ever nibbled a piece of dark chocolate? That's a mouthful of paradox right there: woo, that's *bitter,* and yet there's that *sweetness.* Paradox is that "impossible" moment when you feel both happy and sad, or tired and excited, or passionate and frightened, all at the same time! We teenagers are no strangers to paradox, and yet we, as a society, so readily dismiss it and choose to rely on the straightforward strengths of logic. I spent so long determined to figure out the *one* thing I was feeling, mistakenly thinking I had to exclude everything else to understand how I really felt.

"But wait," I would have to pause and ask myself. "Am I angry or unbelievably surprised and happy? Or, wonder of wonders, am I *all of those things*?" My intuition—the truth in my gut—has helped me to understand paradox.

For example, how do you feel when you have a crush on someone? Or when you think they might like you back? Or how do you feel in that absolutely wild moment when you think you are about to be kissed (or you're about to kiss someone) for the first time? I know that I felt a crazy mix of fear and bouncy excitement—absolutely terrified, with no idea of what to expect, but *never* would I have *not* wanted to answer that phone call or hold the person's hand or kiss someone back. Even if crushes and romance aren't really on your mind, I'm sure you can think of a moment of emotional paradox, perhaps even confusing, heart-wrenching, head-aching emotional paradox. And guess what: if you haven't noticed yet, we teenagers are especially good at having those moments.

A fifteen-year-old daughter from Michigan who came to our workshop had something to teach me about paradox. Maddy was a quiet introvert, with soft, neat brown hair and a monkey-shaped backpack. Halfway through the workshop, she still barely said a word, knees tucked under her chin as she sat in the circle next to her mom. But her eyes darted avidly from face to face as mothers and daughters began to share their stories. Divorce had quickly emerged as a common thread among the group, with more than two-thirds of the families in the beginning, middle, or end of a difficult divorce. Slowly Maddy raised her hand and began to share about the ups and downs of her parents' divorce when she was six. "I was really young, but I remember them fighting and fighting and fighting—sometimes yelling and even throwing things, like books, across the room. When they separated, I didn't really know *what* to feel, because it was all so complicated. I was sad, and I was scared, but I was also so relieved and almost happy—just because they weren't in the same house anymore." There's a paradox: Maddy's feelings of immense sadness and a touch of fear at her parents separation and yet, at the same time, intense relief that the fighting had pretty much ended. As she continued to speak, another paradox emerged: Maddy is *happy* that this *sad* event happened, because her parents are both in a better place now, however complicated it still makes her feel sometimes. And such paradoxes are not *wrong;* they're just the way life works sometimes.

Another workshop daughter, Brooke, a thirteen-year-old girl from Chicago who jumped up and down when she was excited, once perfectly described her paradoxical relationship with her mom: "It's like she's the absolutely most embarrassing thing in my life. She makes me so frustrated that I just want to *scream* and tear my hair out. But at the same time, I really, really love her, and I'm so grateful for all the time and energy she puts into raising me! I guess sometimes she just knows exactly what I need to hear to feel better, and she makes *the* best chocolate chip cookies. But then I feel so guilty because I'm embarrassed of her and mean to her ALL THE TIME!" I think I actually started to laugh, because Brooke's frustrated, loving, paradoxical situation with her mom was *exactly* how I had felt when I was about thirteen and how I still feel sometimes at age nineteen.

Next time you've got that mixed-up feeling of being without a category to classify yourself, stop and let go, just for a moment, of that logical part of your brain that says, "Okay, now, snap together. Let's evaluate this rationally." Instead, let the paradox, the apparently conflicting realities, exist. Just let them all *be*. Whether it is a "dark night of the soul" or a "dark night in the woods" of your own bed—whether it is being surrounded by homework, fighting with your family, doubting a friend, or questioning yourself—it is rarely *simple*. Much more often it is an intrinsically human paradox. And trusting yourself, listening to your gut, and the voice of your doll in your pocket, is the way out into the sunshine of a new day.

Sometimes, when events, people, or natural disasters overwhelm us, we need (or at least I need) a reminder that our lives are indeed in our own hands. Although often used interchangeably, *fate* and *destiny* have, in fact, two quite different definitions. Did you know that?

DEFINE: Fate

The development of events beyond a person's control;
from the Latin *fatum*, meaning "that which has been spoken";
also, popular characters in Greek and Roman myths—
the three Fates who spun, measured, and cut the life spans of humans

---

The way I see it, fate is the life we are given: the parents we are born to, the house we grow up in, the school we attend, the older sibling who tosses us over a couch, the younger sibling who "borrows" our sweaters, the grandparents who know how to listen (or never seem to listen), the color of our natural hair, the age we get our period, our bone structure (tall, wide hips, and so on), the size of our boobs, the curve of our thighs, and so on. Fate is Vasilisa's mother's death, and her father's marriage to a new woman, and her being sent off into the dark woods—all of which she hardly could have avoided.

But destiny is a different thing altogether.

DEFINE: Destiny

The events that will happen in a person's future,
as determined by the living actions of a web of individuals—
most especially the willful participation of the individual;
from the Latin *destinare*, meaning "to make firm, or establish"

The way I see it, destiny is what we make of life: It is how we approach the fate that has been handed to us. It is the way we choose to deal with our imperfect parents, the friends we reach out to, the classes we focus on at school, the statement we make when we walk out of our bedroom door in the morning (BAM! Check out *these* shoes!), the quality of food we put into our bodies, the way we start a conversation with a stranger, the way we look at a fresh day—from our bed, out the window, into the morning air. Destiny is how Vasilisa chose to approach the challenges thrown in her path—death, loneliness, new family, betrayal. And it is the lessons she learns in the darkness of the woods and in the confines of a crotchety old witch's hut. Destiny is what she, and we, *make* of our lives.

So now I want to ask you some new questions. I want you to really think about them. Then pull out a pen and paper (or a journal) and free-write just the first thing that comes to your head:

- What is your fate so far, and what would you like your destiny to be?
- What are you going to *choose* to do with this one big life of yours?

Listen to the doll, choose the path, and look out for sunrise. This is *daughtering*—living our own lives authentically, using our intuition, so that we can live our relationship with our mom the same way.

2

Big Red Ideas

....

What would happen . . . if suddenly, magically, men could menstruate and women could not? The answer is clear—menstruation would become an enviable, boast-worthy, masculine event: Men would brag about how long and how much. Boys would mark the onset of menses, that longed-for proof of manhood, with religious ritual and stag parties.

—GLORIA STEINEM
"If Men Could Menstruate," *Ms.* magazine, 1978

HAVE YOU EVER HEARD THIS quote before? It's from an essay by the famous and fabulous Feminist (yes, capital "F") Gloria Steinem. I put it here, at the opening of this chapter, because I want it to *provoke* deep thought and maybe even action in you. This chapter is about WOMEN and the baggage and beauty that comes with being one or becoming one in our society.

In chapter 1, we talked about fear, overwhelm, dark nights of the soul (and dark nights in the woods—or in science class or alone in our own beds—wherever they may strike us). And we acknowledged something crucial along the way: our intuition (that doll in our pocket) is one of the most essential keys to finding our own way in life. When we feel the most confused (about friends, romance, or mom) or stuck in a "paradox" of emotion, that knowing in our gut can be our best friend.

Well, keep a tight hold on that doll of yours (she will always come in handy), because I want to move one short jump from fear to *awkward*. I plan—without shame—to dwell on those topics that always seem to come with large, flashing, RED lights (beware, beware, *socially unacceptable*, **AVOID!**). I'm sure you can think of a couple. And an exploration of "womanhood" is hardly real without a collection of awkward pitfalls. But you see, we're tough girls, and we're braver than all that. And sometimes, just sometimes, the very ideas that we can't talk about *without* blushing furiously are the most important ones to talk about if we want to become stronger. Why is there this cruel law of the universe? Oh gosh. Read on!

This chapter is about the lovely inheritance that comes with the complex concept of womanhood, of which all of us female-sexed beings are unavoidable inheritors (whether it thrills us, confuses us, or makes us sick to our stomachs). I believe that it is impossible to dig into the life of a teenage girl—or the relationship of a *daughter* to a mother—without opening up this can of (pretty, pink) worms. This chapter discusses four main Big Red Ideas. (Drum roll, please):

- Periods (first ones, especially)
- Celebrating the moment you become a woman
  (Is there one??)
- Red tents (I'll explain)
- The real "herstory" (behind you and the women
  in your family)

These ideas or concepts or subjects (as awkward or desperately uncool as they may seem to some) are each and every one special to me—*sacred*, even (yes, I'm gonna use that "mother" word). They deal with the values and questions that my twenty-one-year-old camp counselors, Melissa and Sophia, taught me to ponder and love when I was only thirteen. They are a sacred teen-girl legacy, passed on from them to me to YOU, and they have everything to do with *being real* and *realizing the person you want to become*. Maybe these big red ideas (which are, really, too BIG to be neat, too RED to be quiet or polite, and most definitely too ancient to fit any stereotypical definition of "cool") can also be your tools, as they have been mine. They are what I think a teen girl on her way to womanhood *has to know*—or at least has to pause and seriously consider. Dive in! Who knows—one just might inspire you.

I want to start off with a definition. Let's expand our "women" words:

DEFINE: Menarche

A girl's first period; from the Greek words *men*, meaning "month," and *archaios*, meaning "beginning." It is the monthly beginning. Sweet.

Okay, let's be real: most people don't talk about periods, unless it's in code or as an excuse to grumpily complain about the day. But actually to be heard—just, ya know, chatting it up about periods—that's NBD (no big deal)? Most people would rather be caught dead, right?

But let's also face reality: *every* girl and woman has or will have her own first period and her own first-period story. We *can* talk about getting our period without having to blush like crazy, and we *can* chat about starchy tampon dramas without being grossed out (or just pretending to be because everyone else seems to be), and we can even debate national period-length averages around the lunch table without being scared like heck of what someone nearby might think. It's actually kind of fun—and maybe even exciting. (Try it.)

Getting our period is part of who we, as teenage girls and young women, are. All right, we didn't sign up to get it ("Yes, I'd like blood out of my vagina once a month, please!"), but why should we feel ashamed or embarrassed? That's a waste of our energy. And here's my next question (and my fear): If we start believing that our periods are "gross" (or embarrassing or a curse or . . . you fill in the blank), how long until we accept that our bodies (the things that produce our periods), and even we ourselves, are "gross"? We need to fix the world's take on periods, starting with our friends, our families, and ourselves. And we can begin by sharing our stories.

When the topic of periods comes up in my workshops—after the girls stop blushing and start talking—one of the biggest issues that comes up is BOYS: How do you deal with talking about periods around the mostly uninformed other sex? I remember Mary, a dirty-blonde soccer captain and tree-frog enthusiast who had come from Delaware with her mom for the workshop. She raised her hand at a pause in the circle's chatter. "I don't have a problem with getting my period or anything," she said. "It's just when boys make a joke about it—either calling me a bitch if I happen to disagree with them (like I'm grumpy 100 percent of the time because of my period), or making some kind of gross, stupid blood joke. It sucks." There were nods of consensus around the room; clearly Mary wasn't alone. So what do you do? Talk, I said. Let someone know if he (or she) pisses you off. Let people know when they're saying things that have no basis in biological fact. And help them. Yes, help out those poor, uninformed boys. (Do you think their parents sat them down for a nice, informative chat about girls' periods?) Some will still be jerks (that's nothing to do with their being male; it's just their particular personality), but the reality is that a lot of boys are just clueless and actually wouldn't mind knowing the simple truth behind the lies they may hear.

Brianne hid the fact that she'd gotten her period—from her mom and everyone else—for four months. Lily didn't get it until her senior year of high school. Marlene got it at home and called to tell me because she was too excited to wait until school the next day! Emma got it on vacation in Africa with her grandmother (who didn't believe her when she came out of the bathroom to tell her). Kristin got it in a friend's bed at a sleepover. Regardless of whether it was the most embarrassing sequence of events EVER or a small and exciting gem of a moment, rare is the girl who will proudly roll out her first-period story to a listening audience.

Rachel Kauder Nalebuff, the editor of *My Little Red Book* (a *fantastic* must-read collection of first-period stories), says in her introduction that just starting to talk about periods can "help us embrace the awkwardness and thereby end it."[4] Let's take that as a motto for this entire chapter, shall we? And to lead by example, here, for all of you (and the world) to read, is my own story:

The Rusty Dot

I was the girl who thought she was never going to be a woman. The girl who obsessively checked her underwear, breathless in the bathroom stall, but only ever found the same old nothing. It wasn't just the "secret" red stain on my underpants that I was waiting for—it was everything. You know—all the woman things that went along with the red stain. **I was a gangly giant,** with overlarge feet and splay-footed rubber sneakers. My boobs were officially graded "pancakes" by my best friend, Savannah (in comparison to her envious "apples"). I would have been happy with anything in the realm of fruit. I was fourteen, and frankly things appeared to be getting desperate.

But how do you make something come when it won't? How do you make your uterus shed when it doesn't want to yet?

Why doesn't it want to yet? I read every book on "The Care and Keeping of You" and "My First Period" that I could possibly find. I Googled my heart out on the subject. I wished that there was a food I could eat, like spaghetti, to bring it on. Life would be simpler that way. If you didn't want to get it, you just wouldn't eat spaghetti.

Savannah had already had her period for two straight years. We were the same height, same big hair, same big feet, but one of us was a coltish girl and the other a young woman. She wanted me to get my period even more than I did (if that's humanly possible). I think early bloomers (like my lovely bestie, Savannah) can feel just as conspicuously ODD and hopelessly irregular as the late bloomer (my charming self). When a body changes (or doesn't), there is pretty much no way to hide it: you and your changes are on display. It's **super** easy to feel like the kid with "MENSTRUATING" or "WEARING A BRA" or even "STILL JUST BREAST BUDS" written in red Sharpie on her forehead. Quite honestly, who doesn't feel like that at some point? Pimples? Stretch marks? Braces?

I was fourteen years old. It was March third, a school night, around 11:30 at night. I peed. I examined. And good thing I was a practiced period detective by now, because I swear I would have missed it otherwise: the literal period that was my period. It could have been a rust-colored fleck in the all-natural toilet paper.

"Mom?!" I called.

"What, honey?" she said.

"Did I get my period?" (She is a nurse after all). She examined the toilet paper. I held my breath.

"Where?" she asked.

"Where?! Right there!!" I pointed to the spot of brown/red.

"**CONGRATULATIONS!**" The magic word. The wait was over! Despite the late hour, despite the fact that I had to get up early the next morning for school, I jumped, I spasmed, I shrieked! I tried to fall asleep, I really did, but imagine lying there with all those bubbly **I Am a Woman** thoughts zinging through your head.

The next morning, at 6:30 a.m. sharp, my mom woke me up for school with a carved wooden red rose. At breakfast, I ate a giant bowl full of strawberries with my pancakes (specially prepared for my BIG red day). And I told my dad—**yes,** I did. It was kind of like diving off of a cliff. You hold your breath and just do it.

"Hey, Dad, igotmyperiodlastnight."

"Oh, wow, congratulations, honey. That's great." A smooch on the head.

"So, what classes have you got today? You have that French test?"

And sweet relief . . . back to normal. But quite frankly, I felt like he deserved my honesty. I didn't want to hide things from him and have him hear from my mom, but that didn't mean we had to talk about it, either.

At school, walking down the deserted eighth-grade hallway with Savannah, I took her hand and whispered, "I got my period last night." She squealed and insisted on rubbing my belly to feel the "swollen ovaries" that "always" make a little bump on the first day you get your period. All day I had this secret, and I doled out the joyful knowledge like a present to my friends. They didn't have to know it was this little rusty dot or that I had almost missed it.

I didn't want everyone to know, of course. I didn't want a women's circle or a party (though, trust me, my mom did ask). I just wanted a hug, a rose, strawberries, and a day where I felt like a princess. It was all going to be okay, because I, Eliza Alden Reynolds, was MENSTRUATING.

My story is a positive one. I was looking forward to my first period, and when the day arrived, it was an "event," something to be celebrated (in my own small, personal way) and remembered. Some first-period stories, like my mom's, are what she calls "nonevents."

She doesn't quite remember it—there was no one to share the moment with and no one to explain what the heck you did with the pad. For my mom, the very nonexistence of her first-period story is sad. Do you know your mom's first-period story? Or your grandma's? Why not ask them to tell you? They each have one, that's for sure.

I think the real secret, whether the issue is periods or anything else where there is awkwardness, is that for some mystical reason, just talking (yes, just a simple conversation) can make it ridiculously better. Talking without fear (or even with fear) about something that makes you uncomfortable takes the power away from the subject and gives that power to you. If you aren't embarrassed, chances are that others won't be, either. Then again, they might be. But if you take pride in, say, the fact that you have finally gotten your period, or that sometimes you think about what happens when you die, or that you *love* to read, or that you would still rather sleep with a light on, or that your period snuck up on you and you need a darn tampon, the only one blushing in her (or his!) own aura of awkwardness will be the other person. You can just smile and feel a bit sorry for them. They are the ones with the problem now, not you.

The idea of talking about things that make you feel awkward extends beyond something as universal and natural as periods. In a small circle of daughters within our weekend workshop, Kelly, a fourteen-year-old redhead and video-game lover from New York City, shared the mortifying moment when, at the beginning of her freshman year of high school, a rumor had started about her and one of her new guy friends, Stephen. People started saying that they liked each other, that they were dating, or that when they got together to do homework after school, they were actually just making out. But none of it was true! They just did their Algebra II homework together sometimes. Stephen was so embarrassed that he stopped talking to Kelly, and the next day her friend Melissa had to tell girls off in the bathroom for calling Kelly a "girl who puts out," supposedly in exchange for help with math homework (though, apparently, Kelly was *great* at math). A week later, Kelly couldn't stand it anymore, and she talked to Stephen right up front about it, pushing past the awkwardness. They talked about how embarrassed they were that everyone was assuming things about them. In the end, it didn't matter what people thought, it mattered that they had talked to each other and knew what was really up.

In the teenage years, I got REAL fed up with feeling awkward. And the secret is: You can fight it! You can free up the stories, questions, and conversations that no one else seems to have the ovaries (that is, the female balls, ahem) to deal with. Liberate those imprisoned first-period stories! Liberate them at the cafeteria table during lunch. Liberate them on the bus home from school. Liberate them in the kitchen. Does your best friend have a story yet? Does she prefer tampons or pads? Does she get bad cramps? How long does her period last? If she hasn't gotten it yet, how does she feel about getting it? Ask! Take away that gosh-darn mysteriously awkward power that we've conferred upon periods. And beyond that, liberate yourself to talk about what is *really* on your mind.

My next "woman" word:

DEFINE: Initiation

A celebration or ritual of sorts in which a group acknowledges that one of its members has changed roles within the group; a process or event that signifies a transformation in which the initiate is, metaphorically speaking, "reborn"

Now that big red subjects have been opened, I want to ask you some questions: When exactly does a girl become a woman? I mean, is there a literal moment? When will you know? Is it the very instant you get your period, right there on the toilet seat? Is it when you turn eighteen or when you get a tattoo or a piercing? Or is it when you graduate from college? How about when you get married or get a "real" job or have kids? Or . . . maybe, gosh, do some people never really get there?

Modern society has no solid way of acknowledging when a girl becomes a woman—or when a boy becomes a man, for that matter. We teens are in this state of what feels like almost constant, never-ending transition. Girl? Tween? Teen? Young woman? How will we have any idea when we are Women? All *I* know is that I'm not one now.

Marking people's transitions through life with ceremony is an old and powerful tradition. These celebrations or rituals are called *initiations.* A simple example in our lovely, everyday modern lives is marriage: the unmarried are regularly initiated into their married roles, usually in some sort of semireligious ceremony involving a big white dress, lots of family, and a whopping large cake.

With this initiation idea in mind, getting your first period does seem to be the best, unsung opportunity for girls to get some props for who they are just at a time when, let's face it, our confidence in our bodies, emotions, home lives, and school lives could use a little boost. For example, in the Asante tribe of Ghana, West Africa, a girl who has just gotten her period is seated on a throne and given gifts of music, dance, and food. The Yurok Indians (originally from California) believe that while a woman has her period, she should be in isolation because she is at her most powerful and shouldn't be bothered with talking to men or going about her ordinary life. Pretty cool idea, in my opinion. I mean, I love the guys in my life, but I also love the idea of my period being a time for me to focus on my own self. I love the idea of my period as not merely a monthly pain but also a monthly source of power. Wrap your head around that one!

The idea is that if we were initiated—if our growing up, our growing out (literally here—boobs, butts, bellies, the like) were celebrated—then we would be more confident in ourselves as young women. If on the day that the first rusty spot or scarlet splotch appeared on our underwear, we were hugged, given a bouquet of red roses, treated to our favorite foods for dinner, and encouraged to feel special, as if our most important of birthdays had arrived without our planning for it, we would be more comfortable in ourselves as young women.

There are also terrible, painful initiations that still occur in our modern world, though slightly less so than in the past. For example, in some African countries, including Kenya, Somalia, and Ethiopia, among others, it is still a common practice for a young teenage girl to experience genital cutting, in which parts of her labia, clitoral hood, and clitoris are removed, often without medication to numb the pain. Specific practices vary from tribe to tribe and country to country. There are now laws in place to stop genital cutting, but enforcement is still an issue, as these behaviors have deep cultural and religious histories. (If you'd like to know more or be involved in giving girls the option to end this form of violent initiation, see the work of Tostan.org or Vday.org).

But whether the change into womanhood is a celebration or a trauma, here in America, we are pretty much *uninitiated*. The Jewish tradition of a bat mitzvah (or bar mitzvah for a boy) at age thirteen is the closest many have in this modern world of ours. So, what can the rest of us do for initiation? Well, we can take it into our own hands. That's what my friends and I have done at least.

My older friend Julia had an afternoon picnic party and invited the most important women and girls in her life. She called it a "period party." I remember my eleven-year-old self—blue headband, red glasses—sitting in that circle, listening in amazement to each person share about womanhood and what they saw in Julia. Emma went out to dinner in New York City with just her mom (after Emma got back from Africa with her grandmother, that is). Barbara stayed home from school and in bed all day, reading and being cozy. As I said, I got little red presents from my mom, a hug from my dad, and my favorite pancake breakfast with strawberries.

You can celebrate your period, too. You really can. And you can do it in the way that *you* want to do it, not the way that your mom or someone else suggests. It's your big milestone, after all. Even if you've already gotten your period, it's *never* too late to celebrate. It is not a secret that it always feels good to mark the meaningful things that happen to us with a celebration (even if it's a private celebration). This may be especially true of the one thing that says most clearly (biologically, at least) that you are on your way to womanhood: your period. What would make you feel proud, instead of embarrassed, of being a menstruating girl? What would make you, a year from now (or thirty years from now), remember and smile about the day that you celebrated your first period?

So celebrate yourself. Celebrate your *whole* self.

DEFINE: Goddess

Yes, we may all know the word. We may even know its etymology as a derivative of the masculine "God." But check out these other definitions:
1. A woman of extraordinary beauty and charm
2. A greatly admired or adored woman

In every workshop I teach with my mom, we build a literal red tent in the far corner of our large teaching room. It has four posts and a peaked roof in the center. We drape the entrance with sparkling, hand-embroidered Indian saris and cover the floor inside with a red carpet and pink and gold throw pillows. At the back of the tent, we make a small altar—it's really just a little table that we cover with swishy red fabric and decorate with miniature statues of goddesses: Kali, the Indian goddess of destruction in the service of creation; Venus, the Roman goddess of love; Quan Yin, the Buddhist goddess of compassion; the Virgin Mary, the Christian mother goddess; and many more who find their places on this lovingly decorated spot.

We lay out soft blankets and nice-smelling hand lotions. We supply big pads of white paper and plenty of pastels. By the end of the weekend, the inside of the tent is papered wall-to-wall with new goddesses: the Goddess of Soccer, the Goddess of Bad Hair Days, the Goddess of Soup Kitchens, the Goddess of Not Being Afraid of Cranky People, the Goddess of the Evil Bikini . . . you get the idea. In fact, I'm sure you can imagine a few real-world goddesses yourself who could use a shout-out.

Our red tent is inspired by the book *The Red Tent*, by Anita Diamant, which gives a voice and a story to the biblical character Dinah (who is named in the Bible, but speaks not one word). In *The Red Tent*, Dinah's family honors the women of her tribe by stopping their nomadic wanderings for one week out of every four in order to allow the women to rest while they have their periods. Once a month, they build a red tent, and all of the menstruating women disappear into it to share the stories and wisdom of the tribe. And for one whole week, the men guard the women while they spend time together. (As an aside: Although *The Red Tent* is a beautiful book, its story arc has many elements of violence. With absolutely no condescension, allow me to say that it's a great read to look forward to in your late teens.)

In our mother-daughter red tent, we do not get together to bleed, that's for sure. Instead, in our red tent, we snuggle and get cozy. We nap. We read. We light nice-smelling candles and rub each other's hands and feet with fragrant lotions. We practice taking care of ourselves. We check out of the achievement-oriented agenda of our brains and give our bodies a little well-earned rest, relaxation, and LOVE. We get to *be* without any kind of goal or checklist, without anything that we need to *do*.

Some people take the red tent home with them. (Not literally, of course—we can't have people snipping off pieces of our precious tent!) Instead, they set aside a corner of an attic or a bedroom or an office to become a red tent, or sometimes it's just a red carpet and two cozy pillows. I painted part of my bedroom red and remade my bed with red sheets, red blankets, red pillowcases, and pink throw pillows. It's kind of like childhood forts taken to the *whole* next level. A red tent is a refuge, a haven from everyday life; it is a place to laugh, cry, think, and write. To relax. A red tent is a place for YOU time.

So, go ahead, try it. Scavenge your house for cozy red pillows and blankets! Find a candle and an image of a goddess or goddess-like woman who inspires you. What the heck—go out and draw ten goddesses, even if you can't draw for your life (like me)! Go out and buy (or ask your mom to buy) a little red lantern or a pink and red throw pillow or two.

Build your own red tent. It's a space for your REAL self, your authentic self, to hang out. And, who knows, you might just invite your mom in, too.

DEFINE: Matriline

Literally a "mother line"; one's matriline is one's mother and her mother and her mother ad infinitum—one's nearly infinite line of mothers

---

"I am Eliza, the daughter of Sil, which is short for Priscilla, who is the daughter of Alden, who is the daughter of Priscilla, who was the daughter of Anabel, who was the daughter of Anna. And that's all I know." I look around the circle at the assorted mothers and daughters as the mother on my left begins and then her daughter repeats their names after her. As her daughter blushes and stumbles through the names, I try to peek into her mind. "Why the heck are they making us do this weird introduction?" I imagine her asking herself. I understand her question, because I used to think this exercise was . . . well, let's just say I was humoring my mom. But we do this introduction because everyone has at least one *matriline* and sometimes maybe more, because belief, adoption, or marriage can give you another matriline—cool! More often than not, we know much less about the history (or herstory) of the women in our family than we do about the men. This is something I know I want to change.

Some of what you inherit from your matriline is physical: What size are your boobs gonna be when they're fully grown? What shape will your butt be when you're forty-five? When will you get your first period? A pretty good answer to these questions is right there in the genetic legacy of your biological mother. Physically, at least, it seems to be true that the apple never falls far from the tree. Other than getting more exercise or eating more healthily than our mothers, all we can do to change our body is . . . hmm, nothing. Just accept it as it is—that's a huge lesson right there (more to come in chapter 4).

But there is something else in a matriline, something we girls know intuitively, something *we've* been talking about with our girlfriends before neuroscientists and psychologists got around to proving it. There is a psychological and emotional layer of our matrilineal inheritance. Plainly speaking, sometimes we have inherited these fantastic gifts, and sometimes we get some baggage to deal with. More often than not, it's both. We girls have realized this for centuries, especially when the baggage is more obvious than the gifts. "Whoa," we might say today. "She's got a lot to deal with—her mother is a piece of work." But what about the idea that we've *all* got a psychological inheritance down the matriline and that our job is to figure out what that inheritance is?

Now excuse me for a moment while I state the obvious: Your mother is a daughter. She will never stop being one, even if her mom has passed on. Just as you will never, in your heart of hearts, stop being a daughter—it's just a fact of life. Your mom was a baby daughter (in diapers, crying, teething), a "terrible two" daughter, a third-grader-with-a-science-project daughter, a middle-school daughter and, yes, as she's probably told you a million times, a *teen daughter* (you may have even seen pictures of this stellar stage of life; if not, GO LOOKING!). All of those phases are part of the package that she is now. Your mom, too, is a work in progress.

So what did your mom inherit from *her* mother? Her hair or maybe her eyes or the way she tells a joke? Her thighs? Hands? I know that in my family, we talk about this all the time, usually sentimentally, sometimes with a "Thank *goodness* I have her hair," and sometimes with a "Gosh, *why* did I get her teeth?" If you're adopted, the realities of genetic legacy are more of a puzzle. Not knowing some of the hard facts about your physical legacy—things like risk factors for certain diseases—can be frustrating, or even more than frustrating. But as far as the moment of *now,* your own physical developments are one key to understanding what your biological mother's are, and have been. And even if you cannot see yourself in your adoptive mother's physicality, perhaps the two of you can compare, explore, giggle, and learn from each other's different physical experiences.

What was your mom's *psychological* inheritance? And here I'm talking about the mom who raised you. What was your mom's relationship like with *her* mom? Did her mom listen to her? Did her mom cuddle with her? Did her mom yell at her? Did her mom tell her she was beautiful or say the words, "I love you"? Did they shop together? Go on walks together? Cook together? Do homework together? What I'm getting down to is this: What pattern for mother-daughter relationships was *your mom* given?

The newest research in psychology shows that stuff like this *is* actually internalized. For example, if a mom happens to have a problem with her own body (and I'm talking a psychological problem, such as always going on diets, making comments about her weight, feeling emotionally uncomfortable with the way she looks, even bordering on being totally obsessed with it), it is very likely that her daughter (even totally against her will) is going to have a similar problem with her own body. At the very least, her mom's body baggage will be something the daughter has to *work* to set down. Let's be real about the bigger picture: mothers have a big effect on us daughters, maybe more than we'd like to admit.

My good friend Kate's mom was physically and verbally abused by her own mother. When Kate was seventeen years old, she was the soft-spoken, strong-willed head of her high school's peer counseling group, and she was frank and open with me about her mom's experiences. "I know that it was obviously really hard for my mom and that she's worked really hard to have a good relationship with me," she says. "I guess to compensate in some ways and to do it right. Sometimes I feel like she's almost trying to be too close to me, even as I go off to college. It's like she's scared of us not being close." Kate's mother is a sweet, hardworking woman (granted, this is from my somewhat removed teenage-friend point of view), and she is *devoted* (understandably) to giving her daughter the mother-daughter relationship she never had. That is her matrilineal baggage to carry, baggage that she has worked with personally in therapy for twenty years so that she can be strong enough not to pass it on to her daughter. It may not even have been the abuse itself that she was afraid of passing on, but rather what was left over: the pain, anger, and sadness that she carried with her as a result of the abuse.

There are certainly less traumatic stories. Tory is sometimes critical of her friends' silly antics, just as her mom is critical of Tory's bouncy energy. Monika makes comments about her body, just as her mom makes comments about her own. Crystal doesn't hesitate to talk to the blushing new girl at school, just as her mom is never afraid to strike up a cheery conversation with a stranger in the grocery line.

So here's the thing: your mom was a teenage daughter once herself—as fully, energetically, and honestly as you are one now. What is your mom passing on to you? What is your psychological inheritance? Take a moment to actually think about it. Name one thing, just one, that you want to inherit from your mom (like a certain skill she has, a character trait, or a way of seeing the world). And then name one thing you consciously don't want to inherit, because the open secret is *once we're conscious of our inheritance, we can actually choose what to keep, what to let go, and how we want to live in the world every day.*

For myself, I don't want to inherit the way my mom is always late—whether it's to pick me up or to arrive for a meeting. I try to do things differently out of respect for the person I am going to meet and to avoid having to make those red-faced, perspiring-with-anxiety apologies. But I definitely *do* want to inherit my mom's optimism and good mood in the face of crappy situations. Like how she laughed when I picked up the wrong suitcase at the airport, and she had to wear the same outfit for an entire workshop-leading weekend. She's great that way, as I'd like to be once I can figure out how to outgrow my crazy, unpredictable grumpy mood swings that she seems never to fall prey to (or maybe she once did, like me?).

So grab a journal or a piece of paper from the printer. (Whatever's easier, closer, faster!) Write down at least three psychological things that you *don't* want to inherit from your mom. (Yes, dear girl reader, I mean *actually* do this!). Below that, write down at least three psychological things that you absolutely *do* want to inherit. And if you're tempted to spend more time writing about the things that you don't want to inherit (it's okay, we all have those feelings sometimes), you might want to consider giving equal time to the things you do want to inherit—just a thought. Create a time for finding the positive.

Save what you've written. You may or may not want to revisit this list from time to time in the future. *If we're conscious about these things, we can choose.* Remember (and don't ever forget): it's your life, not your mom's.

3

Heart Trust

....

*Just because you've got the emotional range
of a teaspoon doesn't mean we all have.*
—HERMIONE GRANGER TO RON WEASLEY
Harry Potter and the Goblet of Fire, by J. K. Rowling

WELCOME TO THE CHAPTER ABOUT all things emotional: nervous
butterflies in your stomach, crying for "no reason," flirty text
messages, snuggling, what falling in love *means,* and how being
smart can include knowing what you feel and what to do about it.
This chapter is also about things that piss you off (sometimes for
no apparent reason, sometimes for a lot of gosh-darn good reasons) and about things that make you feel totally overwhelmed,
grumpy, gloomy, and unable to get *anything* done because you're
stuck obsessing. Daughtering requires that we learn to trust our
hearts—something that is not often "taught" in a traditional
sense, but a lesson that we must take up or risk being lost in the
dark woods of Vasilisa's wanderings. Too often these wanderings
are our own complex emotional web. The most important relationships in our lives, whether with our best of friends, romantic

relationships, siblings, or parents, require that we learn how to be our best, strongest, and most authentic self. In this chapter, we're going to tackle just that.

Emotions are powerful things, especially for us teenagers. Have you ever had a total mood swing? I know I have, and frankly the speed with which I can switch from gleeful to pissy is *rather* impressive. And for the most part, we've been told (as "overemotional" teens) by our pop culture of TV shows, movies, and magazines, and our society of teachers, cool kids, and whomever else we happen to listen to, that emotions are things that will *confuse* us, make us *weak*, and make us *crazy*. So, therefore, logically, the best thing for us to do is, what? Avoid emotions altogether!! Duh.

Not true!

Emotions are what *connect* us to other people. They are the guides that help us *understand* our reactions and what makes us happy or sad (or crazy!). For example, when I walk into my English teacher's office to meet about a paper, and I feel the familiar knot in my stomach, I know I must be nervous—but why? I did well on the paper. So I have learned to force myself to relax and try to get over my irrational anxiety about authority figures. Shoulders back, chin up, Eliza! You've got this. Or when I break down in tears at 8:00 on a school night, overwhelmed by my schoolwork and sad about the fight I got into with my friend Sarah, I've learned that it's about time to take a break. I find a box of tissues, and I get in bed with my diary and hold myself until the tears are over. Once I've cried out my sadness—my fear of losing my friend, made so much worse by the math test I have tomorrow—and I've scribbled away about *why* it happened and *what* I'm going to do about it next week, I begin to feel calm. It's going to work itself out tomorrow; now it's time to focus on one thing at a time.

Learning about your own emotions is like strengthening a muscle that we all have but that is often underworked. If you don't develop your emotional "strength," then yes, you will become weak and brittle (easy to break!) in this world. And frankly, if we don't deal with emotions directly and listen to what they have to say, they *will* overwhelm us.

I have come to love my emotions, even though sometimes they seem to torment me with their unpredictability and the power they have to totally flood me when I absolutely *least* need it (during final exams, for example). But mostly, my emotions and the way they run their course are now pretty familiar to me. I generally (um, usually) more or less understand the silly, egotistical, reactionary way they seem to operate. I find some kind of comfort and, oddly, a feeling of power in knowing and understanding them; they help me make sense of my place in the world around me.

DEFINE: Smart

Characterized by quickness and ease of learning;
capable of independent and apparently intelligent action

When we say that someone is *smart*, what do we usually mean? Oh gosh, they've got like *such* good grades, they think superlogically, and I'm sure they have an IQ score that's through the darn roof. As a society, we do seem to define intelligence in terms of basic *academic intelligence*—in other words, what you learn in school, what you spend your afterschool hours doing homework on, and what gets you into college. But I think we need to redefine *smart*, because we all know that this one definition is way too narrow. Actually, research has shown that there are many different types of intelligence—at least ten, in fact! We have (or have a frustrating lack of) body "kinesthetic" intelligence, musical intelligence, spiritual intelligence, naturalist intelligence (how nature smart we are—knowing how to forage for food, for example, or to navigate by the pattern of the stars), and even spatial intelligence (a type of "picture smart," for those who are primarily visual thinkers).

Body intelligence, for example, is the kind of *smart* possessed by athletes or dancers who naturally know how to use their bodies (hand-eye coordination, anyone?) and who understand what their bodies need in order to stay healthy and perform. Body intelligence is something that some people (that star basketball player or field-hockey player at your school) seem to have from birth. But we can all work at developing it. For better or worse, we all know how much body intelligence we have. Right?

Another kind of intelligence is spiritual intelligence, where someone has the ability to know and explore that eternal, universal part of ourselves that some call "soul." Someone who is spiritually intelligent seeks and often finds meaning in something bigger than herself—and, yes, this can be through religion or spiritual practice, or even through a love of animals or nature. Spiritually intelligent people often find themselves exploring some of life's BIG questions—like what happens when you die, or what does it mean to be a "moral" human being. (What do *you* think it means?)

And then we have *emotional intelligence*. Yes, a type of intelligence that has to do with *just* your emotions! Here's how it's defined:

DEFINE: Emotional Intelligence

The ability to identify, assess, and manage the emotions of one's self and others in a healthy and productive manner

Someone who is emotionally intelligent knows how other people are feeling, knows how they themselves are feeling, has a strong sense of empathy (being able to *feel* what other people are feeling, not just understand it), and has good communication skills. Possessing emotional intelligence—being "heart smart"—is finally being acknowledged (or perhaps it is only something that we are remembering after centuries of having forgotten it) as a desirable trait in people, whether you want to hire them, date them, or elect them to be your president. Don't you want someone whose skills go beyond just logical choice-making? We certainly can't *daughter* without it.

Who is an example of *somebody* in your life who is emotionally intelligent? Pause for a second and identify *one* person. Some people just seem to be naturally good at emotional intelligence, but we can all work on it. Within my family, my Gram was famous for her emotional intelligence and her ability to just authentically *connect.* Consider taking this person as a "heart smart" role model.

Ideally, emotional intelligence develops with maturity, once we leave the childhood years and the ups and downs of the teenage mood swings. But reaching adulthood is no assurance that you will have developed your emotional intelligence. Unfortunately, there are many "adults" who do not recognize their own emotions or the emotions of those around them, and who approach situation after situation with emotional immaturity. It's a disappointing lesson to learn that in some ways you may be more *emotionally intelligent* than a person you looked up to as a child.

My friend Carrie had an experience like this, an experience that broke down her illusion about adulthood, specifically about her dad. I met Carrie at the first workshop I ever taught. She was fourteen, with wiry black hair and bright orange pants. In the years that have followed, she has become one of my workshop assistants. Carrie's parents divorced when she was seven, and she spent the next ten years moving back and forth from house to house every week. She had to ask for two different math textbooks for the two different houses, she had two different sets of clothes, and two different ways she had to act, because her parents expected different things from her. In essence, she felt that she had to be two different people.

When she was seventeen, she realized that the constant moving, the constant splitting of who she was, was driving her crazy, and she told her dad that she didn't want to live with him anymore (she *couldn't*). He was furious and stopped talking to her for an entire year. Needless to say, it *sucked*. She alternately felt guilty and then pissed off at her dad and then just sad because of this giant rift between them. It was a time of anguish. (I think she would agree that that's not too strong a word.) Then slowly, ever so slowly, she realized that he just wasn't able to manage his emotions as an "adult" should do or to truly understand her emotions. In a way, *she* had to be the adult in the relationship. Now they meet for dinner once a week, and their relationship is the best it's ever been. Carrie tells me, quite simply, that he treats her like a "real person now, and not a kid who is basically like property to be moved back and forth." I think one of the biggest lessons I ever learned growing up was the reality that all grown-ups aren't all grown-up, and a lot of this has to do with emotional intelligence. It doesn't mean we have to love these grown-ups any less! But it's an important part of realizing their imperfect humanness, however scary (or relieving) that might be.

As you probably know, approximately half of the marriages in the United States today end in divorce. My mom and I once led a workshop where, by chance, 100 percent of the mother-daughter pairs were in the middle of or had already gone through a painful divorce. Sometimes parents are able to stay friends, and sometimes the families are pulled apart by the situation or the emotional immaturity of one or both of the parents. Sometimes you have to be able to locate the one true self (perhaps an intensely sad, grieving, and pissed-off self) who refuses to be divided between two households, as Carrie did. This takes real emotional strength and intelligence, which is something we must build within ourselves if we are to become mature adults (and maybe not repeat some of the immaturity we find in the generations before us).

Divorce isn't the only kind of break that requires us to be strong. There are breaks in friendships, teams, or relationships that can be terribly difficult to deal with. It's very common to feel stuck between two sides of an emotionally messy situation. In fact, I would say it's probably an experience we've all had in one form or another. You know what I'm talking about? I thought so.

The straight truth is this: emotional intelligence is vitally, majorly, über-*important* for us. How can you go through life seeking happiness without being able to understand and deal with your own emotions? As a teen, this can be especially hard, because our hormones and our still not-completely-developed brains (it's true; they're not) and our bodies are throwing a lot at us all at once. Think about how someone being really grumpy (or just straight-up *mean*) for "no reason" can ruin your day. Now, what if you could read other people's emotions really well and understand that (1) this person may have a very good reason to be in a horrible mood, (2) it really has nothing to do with you (that person is having an emotional reaction, and it's not your fault!), and (3) you should not take it personally. Wouldn't your whole day be so much better? *That* is emotional intelligence. Now you may think, "Gosh, doesn't *everyone* know how to do THAT?" And the simple answer is **no!** Some people have never learned a lesson like this, and the truth of it is, even those like me, who are consciously trying to become more emotionally intelligent, often find it really hard not to get ticked off, guilty, or incredibly sad as a result of someone else's emotional funk.

What if you could effectively communicate *exactly* what you were feeling? What if your friend's crossed arms and pursed lips were never a mystery anymore? What if you could easily understand and accept your emotional paradoxes (as we talked about a bit in chapter 1) without pushing yourself into rigid black-or-white thinking (I can't be guilty *and* relieved about something. I have to choose one!)? This is emotional intelligence. Having a workable relationship with your mom—or with anyone for that matter—requires emotional intelligence; you cannot hope to get what you want and need out of the relationship (that is, you can't hope to *daughter*) unless you truly know what you feel *and* can communicate it. We're absolutely crazy if we think we can enter into the teen and adult years without this vital tool.

How exactly do you work on your own emotional intelligence? We spend almost every day working on our academic intelligence: multiplication tables or short essays, science experiments or history books. We are trained in the various ways we should be working to "succeed" and to be "smarter." But I believe that it's also our job to devote *just* as much time to the study of our own emotional intelligence. The world *needs* emotionally intelligent people: people who care about humanity and what we're doing to the earth as a species, people who are emotionally intelligent leaders, people who run emotionally intelligent businesses and who raise emotionally intelligent children. Think of how many problems could be fixed! So, how do we do this?

Emotions Guidelines

(to be done between math sets)

1. Have you ever noticed that emotions are usually felt somewhere in our bodies? It's crazy! I know that my stomach muscles tie themselves into a knot when I'm nervous. Sometimes I don't even know I'm nervous until my stomach is aching and any desire to eat *anything* is totally gone. I carry my stress in my shoulders (they're tense and almost up to my ears). I carry guilt in my chest and upper stomach, like a weight I can't put down. Anger is in my forehead and my hands (hot and itchy, like there's something just fighting to get out!!). Contentment is in my lower stomach, but excitement is in my upper stomach and my knees (I can't seem to stop jumping!). Figure out where in *your* body *you* feel your different emotions. Write down a list of your observations in your journal. Noticing where different emotions "live"

in our bodies can help us recognize them when our body starts sending signals.

2. Sometimes you know how you feel by becoming aware of a sensation in your body first. When we ignore and repress an emotion, our body often takes it on. Check in with your body regularly. Actively listen (every morning when you wake up and all through the day) to the messages it's telling you. If you've already done step 1 and figured out where in your body you feel your different emotions, this step may come pretty easily to you.

3. The next time you feel an emotion, try to acknowledge it rather than ignore it. Try to understand it. Unpack it. Where did it come from? What started it? That moment of intense feeling might not be the best time to express the feeling (feeling angry doesn't mean you *have* to start yelling, and you might not be in a place where you feel comfortable crying). But at least realize it and take note. Internally wave at your emotion. Perhaps it has something to tell you, something you weren't picking up on before. ("Hey, you. Yes, *you*, fear.")

   One of my favorite poets is Rumi, an ancient Sufi mystic (from thirteenth-century Persia—*that* ancient). He composed a poem about just this topic. I find it amazing that a poem like this—which speaks so strongly to my heart—is over eight hundred years old. Some human experiences (and advice) are timeless!

This being human is a guest house.
Every morning a new arrival.

A joy, a depression, a meanness,
some momentary awareness comes
as an unexpected visitor

. . . .

treat each guest honorably.
He may be clearing you out
for some new delight.

What *I* understand the poem to say (because goodness knows we all interpret words and deep thoughts differently—and that's just fine!) is that every emotion we have is *valid* and has a lesson to teach us (it may be making way for some "new delight"). In a way, we are a human "guest house" for our emotions, and we can choose to welcome them all and get to know them—or else, like strange and uninvited guests, they might make a mess, frighten us, confuse us, and make our lives unexpectedly miserable.

4. It's always okay if we cry for "no reason" (even if people keep on asking, with the best and most *annoying* of intentions, "BUT WHAT'S WRONG?"). Our tears can be the product of schoolwork, fatigue, hormones, family stress, friend stress, extracurricular stress, stress over the future, and just a general overwhelm that sometimes strikes. Sometimes you just can't hold it together anymore, and sometimes we *need* to not be able to hold it together anymore. What I've found is that a good release of all the stress (often, for me, with a good cry with a lot of tissues and later a little bit of writing out my thoughts in my journal) resets my tolerance for it all.

5. Understand the *scientific fact* that the teen years are an emotional roller coaster. It's not just a myth; it's very real—it's where the idea that we're "crazy" comes from! We have hormones pumping through our bodies, our brains aren't fully developed (specifically in the all-important decision-making centers), and our bodies are changing dramatically in a span of just a few years. So cut yourself some slack.

6. Commit to becoming more emotionally intelligent. Find some-one, perhaps a *true* adult, who inspires you with his or her empathy and ability to communicate. Take that person as your role model.

7. Take time to think about, watch, and *feel* the level of emotional intelligence in your family. This can be a huge thing to consider. (And perhaps a little scary? What if you were to find some-thing *missing* in your parents?? ARGH!!) Right now, it may be too difficult for you to fully and accurately assess your family's general level of emotional intelligence. That's okay, because this can be a work in progress. But maybe you can begin to see for yourself some emotional patterns that you are a part of or that seem to storm their way around you. Perhaps it is these very patterns that, consciously or unconsciously, you are inheriting. What patterns does your family have for commu-nication? How do people argue in your family? How do you express sadness?

My own family doesn't yell, and we never have. We sit and dis-cuss rationally. If either of my parents are yelling (or are sitting in stony silence), I get worried, because that is *not* our way. Crying, however, *is* our way—or at least my mom's and my way. My mom cries easily, a trait that I've inherited. Although I do not see this as a weakness, it can be very frustrating, because sometimes the minute I begin to feel an intense emotion, even if it's anger, and confrontation and discussion begin, I start to cry. The waterworks turn on. It's totally out of my control. It's like my body flips an invisible switch, and I have to mumble out my words in between my tears, chest heaves, and running nose. If I'm honest, my mom's tears have always made me slightly uncomfortable—there's something in them that's inherently *scary* to me as her daughter. It's like the base of my existence, my safe, relational haven, has become unstable.

In contrast to my family's teary, quiet-discussion-focused format for arguing, my three college roommates—one is Portuguese American, another is Puerto Rican Honduran, and the third is Russian—all come from families that YELL. (Yes, this can be a cultural thing.) Bernadette tried to explain it to me one day, and what she said pretty much boils down to this: there's a simple rule of arguing in her family—whoever is loudest, wins. Actual *content* is really not important. It seems to me that this could be both satisfying (Just yell it out! *Really* give them a piece of your mind!) and totally *frustrating* ("WHAT are we EVEN fighting ABOUT? Are you even LISTENING?!").

My friend Beth also comes from a family, like mine, that doesn't yell, but they don't cry, either. One of her earliest childhood memories is of breaking down over some childhood catastrophe, like her older brother claiming the swing that she wanted to use. What was her mom's first reaction as she came rushing out of the house? Something to the effect of "Come on, honey, let's go wash you up in the bathroom. Stop that, stop those silly tears. You're fine." Beth's mother helped her five-year-old daughter to become "presentable" again, to pretend no upset had ever happened, and that kind of response in her family still continues today. Beth says she doesn't feel like her mom was trying to *repress* her as a child; she was just showing Beth how to take care of herself and *get over it, stop being hysterical,* which was probably exactly what Beth's mother had been taught by her own mother. Even now, in college, the minute Beth starts to cry, when she's sad or getting into a fight with a friend, she excuses herself and goes to the bathroom to wash her face so she can come back and continue the discussion "rationally," as her dad says. But here's the thing: *Beth can't stand it.* She can't stand that this is what she has been taught. She wants to be able to cry in front of her friends, she wants to be able to feel her feelings and know that it's valid and be able to have a real conversation at the same time. She feels that when she can't be emotionally honest or vulnerable with her closest friends, she is withholding a piece of herself. She feels she can't be truly *intimate*.

Beth, sitting across from me in our school's cafeteria, peeling an orange thoughtfully for dessert, says she is *committed* to getting rid of this emotional inheritance. She doesn't have any anger at her parents for it; she just knows that it *doesn't work for her*. Her strategy is to go into therapy and to do hard, honest work on herself and her old triggers and emotional patterns. She inspires me.

Now for the tricky part of this chapter. I want to talk about love, and what in the world is more confusing than love? The next word starts us off:

DEFINE: Intimacy

Close familiarity or friendship marked by affection, warmth, openness, and confidence in each other; closeness—a feeling of belonging together

Togetherness; when the "you" and "me"
begin to disappear and "us" comes to replace it

When I was thirteen years old, my summer camp counselor, Sophia, was the most intuitive (remember *intuition*?), deepest-feeling twenty-one-year-old I had ever met. (Aptly, *Sophia* is the ancient Greek word for "wisdom.") In fact, she still is one of the wisest lights in my life when I feel my darkest. Whenever Sophia sat teen-camper Eliza down for talks about "love" (which was often), she always prefaced these storytelling sessions (where I sat wide-eyed, heart bouncing, soaking in *every last word*) with the phrase:

> There are only three things I know: trust your gut, listen to your heart, and speak your truth. But this has been my experience . . .

In my memory, this saying has become almost a ritual, as well the *right* introduction to advice on anything as personal as love. What can we claim to *know* about love? I'm not sure there is any ultimate truth, but there is experience, and experience is personal truth, and personal truth is something that I find both good and helpful.

The first time I got married, I was four years old (Dante, in my bedroom); the second time, I was five (Wiley, a Florida wedding); and the third time, I was six (Eliot, in my living room). You know what I'm talking about, right? Those pretend weddings that you act out and that grown-ups think are so cute. Yes, maybe I managed to "get around" a bit, but that's all behind me now.

The first time I had an actual crush on someone, I was ten years old. The first time I had a crush on someone that I actually talked to, I was thirteen years old. Then two months later, he actually started to like me back, and I was so scared that I promptly stopped talking to him. Romance as an *idea* was much safer. The first time I kissed a crush, I was fifteen. And then I fell in love with that crush, who became my boyfriend until I was seventeen. This type of long-term relationship was fairly unique among my group of close friends; in fact, I only had one other friend who had a similar relationship at that age.

There is no "right" time for discovering love, crushes, intimacy, and relationships. Carrie had her first relationship when she was nineteen. For Lucy, it was when she was thirteen. The types of relationships they had were different, of course, because they were at different times in their lives. Mary didn't find someone she wanted to kiss until she was twenty-one. Kristin was a serial dater from the age of fourteen on. Wherever you are on the spectrum—whether *love* is the last thing on your mind, or you have a first crush (and you'd really rather no one knew about your crush), or you have a more long-lasting crush (If ONLY that person liked you back! Maybe you could date?), or you're totally in love (in a relationship or just from afar), or you're in your first long-lasting relationship or your first "dating" experience (which means different things this whole world round), or something else! Whomever you decide to love (and it's totally up to you), there is no "right" or "wrong" based on gender, sexual orientation, or anything else. Love is love.

Romantic love can be fun. It makes us giggle and often turn bright red. It makes our upper stomachs jump and squirm. Sometimes it seems to give *meaning* to what feels like an otherwise DULL existence. Romantic love can feel like that great big sparkle in our lives.

Romantic love can also be painful and sometimes so intense that it *consumes* us; it's ALL we can think about. The flipside of romantic love is hurt (jealousy, rejection, self-judgment, even self-hate). Romantic love can be mean and needy and guilty and sad. Romantic love can drag us down into darkness and away from the things and people that make us happy.

So, there are still only three things I know about romantic love (and life): trust your gut, listen to your heart, and speak your truth. But the few personal simple guidelines that follow have come from my own experience:

1. Do the right thing, even (and especially) if it's really, really difficult. Be honest. Sit down friends or loved ones for hard conversations (as in: *I love you enough to tell you my truth*). If you cannot speak face-to-face with the person you love about the honest truth, then there is an important missing link and a certain rift between you that needs to be crossed. Communication is at the heart of any good relationship (romantic or not); it's the gears that make it grind forward.

   For example, imagine Mckenzie—she's been seeing Louis for about two months now. He's a year older, and they get along really well. They laugh a lot—you know, the same stupid humor (talking in funny accents)—and they have a shared passion for secret-agent movies (James Bond, all the way!). But since last

Tuesday, she's been feeling a little paranoid: Why didn't he text her back right away? And why wasn't he online last night? And in the hall last period, he just waved instead of coming over. What's *wrong*? I have a simple answer to all of Mckenzie's gut-wrenching concerns: *ask him*, face-to-face, if anything is in fact "wrong." You won't know until you ask (and until then, your imagination will play tricks on you that you'll always regret). Even if it's painfully difficult or palm-sweatingly scary—if he's worth it, he'll talk it out.

Or what if, for example, you suddenly, painfully, mind-blowingly, flips-in-your-stomach realize you have a huge crush on your best friend's ex? What the heck do you do? Well, first you check in with yourself. Do you *really* like this person? Is your potential *anything* with them (relationship, kisses, dates, conversations) worth the tensions it might cause in your friendship? Or worth, perhaps, even the end of your friendship? Next, is this crush something that (1) is blatantly, in-your-face obvious or (2) everyone is starting to talk about? If so, your dear friend probably needs to know. Have the ovaries (yes, amended from the obviously inappropriate "balls") to sit down and have the necessary REAL, kind, open, brave talk that you *know* needs to happen with your friend. Your friend could respond in any number of ways. There's the "Great, I'm so happy for you" response (preferable), or the "I guess that's fine" (it's totally not that fine) response, or the "How could you?! I am betrayed and heartbroken" (daggers to your gut) response, or any number of variations in between. The point is, you'll be doing the *right* thing, and you are there in friendship, speaking your truth and listening to your heart. This tip doesn't just apply to negotiating friendship and romantic love. Real, difficult, compassionate conversations are a vital part of an emotionally intelligent life.

2. It is *always* okay to say "NO, that's not what *I* want." You should never have to feel guilty, mean, "bad," or sad for following what YOU genuinely want and need in a situation or a relationship.

Sometimes negative, self-blaming feelings may sneak up on you anyway, but don't follow their advice!

For example, when I was fourteen, one of my best friends, Susie (who was sixteen), had a boyfriend named Julien. About three months into the relationship, Susie realized that she just wasn't into Julien in the same way that he was *crazy* about her. But she wouldn't break up with him. "I don't want to hurt his feelings," she would say. "I'd feel so guilty! I mean, maybe in another month I'll like him again." Susie dated Julien for *six more months,* and the whole of that time, she *could not stand it* when he wrapped his arms around her shoulders. She seemed to spend most of her energy in the relationship just finding ways to avoid kissing him, like running to the bathroom with her girlfriends or going off for something to eat. These silly (and rather cruel) games avoided the *real* issue: she didn't want to be with him anymore! And six months later, when Julien found out, he was more heartbroken that Susie had lied to him for six months than he was that she no longer honestly felt the same way about him.

You should not feel *guilty* or *mean* for speaking your truth (even if it's just "NO"), as long as you speak it as honestly, clearly, and compassionately as you can.

Here's another way to think about saying "no." Imagine you're in a situation in which someone *really* wants to kiss you and the LAST thing you want to do is kiss the person back (maybe you're at that mutual friend's birthday party or sitting by the lake one evening at summer camp). Now, you might be thinking: "What *is* Eliza talking about?? Of COURSE, I would say 'no' if I didn't want to! Of course I would break up the relationship if I didn't like the person anymore! Gosh, who does she think I *am?*" Well, that is great! Super fantastic! And I mean that. But take a moment to pause and remember the painful emotional reality that these situations can involve. It's not nearly as easy to do the right thing when we're in the middle of an awkward situation as it is when we're calmly and comfortably removed from it and just *thinking* about it. And remember, too, that there are even more complex situations that might be arising for you in the next few years. So I believe it's important to keep these no-saying lessons close to your heart.

What if, for example, you are in a relationship with someone you are totally, wholeheartedly in love with, and, as is fairly natural, you feel as if you would do anything to keep this person happy and show just how much you deeply care about him (or her). Then he (or she) decides it's time to have sex. You *know* you are not ready yet. You love this person *so* much, but the idea of being *that* sexual makes you totally freaked out. Maybe you don't feel emotionally ready or maybe you just know that you'd rather wait. But he (or she) keeps pushing, though never forcing you—time after time, letting you know how wonderful it would be if *you* wanted to, also. What do you do? Do you worry that perhaps your "love" may start to love you less? That he or she will think you're silly or "young"? Or that he or she will think that you don't *really* love him or her?

A situation like this is bound to be complex, confusing, and PAINFUL. So *what actually do you do?* Trust your gut, listen to your heart, and speak your truth. It is always right to say "no" when your gut, heart, or truth is telling you "NO, NO, NO" (or maybe even just "No thanks, not quite yet"). And if someone else is not respecting that, then maybe he or she doesn't love you that much anyway. Hmm, interesting.

3. Pay attention to when you start to lose your*self* (the *self* you were able to be *before* the person arrived in your life). If this happens, both celebrate this intensity of love and find little ways to connect back to that independent place in yourself. Maybe there are certain friendships that never fail to put you in touch with "you." Maybe going for a walk in the woods can do this, or sweating hard at the gym, or doing a sport, or writing in your journal, or doing some sort of volunteer work. The point is: remember who *you* are (outside of the relationship "us"), even as who you are keeps changing.

Shakespeare's play *Romeo and Juliet* deals with the kind of losing-yourself-in-love experience that we're talking about, and it was written four hundred years ago! In the tale, two fourteen-year-olds—Romeo Montague and Juliet Capulet, the children of rival families—fall madly in love with each other at first sight. This tragic, beautiful, bloody story shows (among other things) how overwhelming and identity-changing young love can be. Romeo and Juliet risk everything for their love. They lie to their parents, they marry in secret, and, ultimately, when things go very, very wrong for them, they end up committing suicide because of their love. Now, however disconnected their story might be from our reality (I mean, it does take place in Renaissance Italy, when people—kids!—actually did get married at that age), there is still great emotional truth in it—a truth about the "madness" and danger of an intense first love. Why else would we still be teaching it in every high school English class in existence?

So the advice that a wonderfully wise, heart-smart older teenage girl gave to me when I was thirteen I will now repeat, again, to you: *trust your gut, listen to your heart, and speak your truth.* The words were true then, and they are true now. In fact, the older I get, the more incredibly important I find them to be. So remember them. Repeat them to your friends. Live by them.

Talking about love with your mom can be an incredibly difficult, embarrassing, but helpful endeavor. It can quite easily feel like one never-ending loop of miscommunication and frustration. I know that my first serious boyfriend, when I was fifteen, added more conflict and chaos to my family than years twelve through fourteen had together. But if there's one thing I learned, it's this: most moms are *afraid.* They know that love hurts, that discovering your own sexuality is intense, and that forming new romantic bonds often takes you away from your family. How do they know all this? Because they've lived it themselves. If you accept this paradoxically rational and irrational fear of theirs (you *are* going to grow up, no matter what they do), and perhaps even acknowledge it, then you will be *daughtering*, and your life will be all the easier for it (I solemnly swear).

I can promise you one thing: the more radically *clear* you can be about how you feel with your mom, the more you will find common ground. Use your emotional intelligence to your advantage. For example, do you feel like your mom always talks down to you and devalues your romantic relationships as "puppy love" and "not the real thing" ("Oh, honey, when you're older . . .")? Well then, *tell her* the truth of how she's making you feel. Sit her down, just the two of you, and *kindly*, honestly tell her. She may have no idea she's even making you feel uncomfortable.

Or what if your mom has been limiting the amount of time you're "allowed" to spend with your new romantic buddy (call them "boyfriend" or "girlfriend" or "lover-person" or "significant other"—whatever you choose)? Or perhaps she's instated an "open door" policy when they're over? (Oh, Mom! How desperately uncool and frustrating you are!) Well, for one thing, it's your mom's house, and she gets to set the rules. You are still, legally speaking, a minor until the age of eighteen, and, as my mom used to say so memorably to me: "Lize, when you're eighteen and you don't live here anymore, you can make your own choices." Bummer. But then sometimes, though it hurts me a little bit to admit it, I know just how right she was. And there's also this part of me that feels rather lucky that she was watching my back. You know, not all moms are like that. I found that I didn't get anywhere if I yelled, pouted, or gave her the silent treatment. I just confirmed her worst fear—namely, that I was really too young to be entering into this kind of a relationship and making choices for myself. So in your case, I suggest that you take a deep breath, realize she's *scared,* and ask her to talk about it with you. Daughtering is using the tools we have—our intuition, the truth of our inheritance, our emotional intelligence—to build the relationship we want. And being "heart smart" is just about the biggest step.

4

Body Trust

··

Look at that tree. Do you see that tree?

Now look at that tree. (Points to another tree.)
Do you hate that tree 'cause it doesn't look like that tree?
Do you say that tree isn't pretty because
it doesn't look like that tree?

We're all trees. You're a tree. I'm a tree.

You've got to love your body.

Love your tree.

—EVE ENSLER
quoting Agnes, a wise woman in Kenya, in *The Good Body*

WELCOME TO THE CHAPTER THAT is devoted entirely to bodies: to bellies and boobs; to thighs and love handles; and, yes, to upper arms, calves, and butts or any lack thereof (however frustrating or exciting that may be).

I have found that even with our closest friends and family, it can be hard to *really* talk about bodies. Too often it becomes a depressing list of things we don't like or a competition between bodies (whether masked with smiles or right out front). More often, we simply don't talk about our bodies because the topic is too touchy, too sensitive, too painful. Just think, you might say something *wrong* to a friend, or worse, she might make one tiny remark that rubs you the wrong way, and BAM, you carry that feeling around in your stomach like a lump of coal for the next two months ("I look *better* in pants?? Does she mean I *shouldn't* be wearing dresses? Do I look fat or something?"). It's safer to just *avoid* body talk altogether, we tell ourselves. But listen, ladies, let's be honest, our body is ours for life, and it's better to have a good relationship with this lifelong part of ourselves than a not-so-good one. We teenage girls *need* to talk about bodies, and we need to remember to be smart and *kind* about others' bodies and about our own.

Body talk is part of the mother-daughter package. Our moms, whether we like it or not, are our central pattern for how we relate to our bodies—and often, if we're biologically related to them, the shape our actual bodies take. It's part of the "fate" we've been dealt. Now on to the "destiny" part of it—the part we can choose. That's the *daughtering* part.

Bodies are vitally important to this book (a book dedicated to growing our most authentic selves), because, let's go ahead and admit it: the teen years can be *rough* as far as our feelings about our bodies go. The changes that are oh-so-quickly happening (or not happening) are a whole new emotional roller coaster that we get to ride all the way to old age. And hey, sometimes the ride can be a fun one—a pretty lace bra may be a nice new addition to your wardrobe, and that moment when you feel kind of, well, *sexy* for the first time can be really *exciting*. After the teen years, the ride does seem to level out a bit, but very rarely do you see a woman who is just sailing along, at peace with every new change that her body decides to offer her. I mean, take a look at your mom (not to be critical here, but she is the closest candidate for any such examination). Is *she* done with, and has she won, the battle for *body love*? How is she dealing with middle age and menopause? Gracefully? Desperately? Enthusiastically? Humorously? Sadly? Some other way? And what about your grandmas, for that matter?

For us—you, me, and all of our peers—the teen years are the beginning of a new kind of relationship, an emotional and psychological one, with our own body. So we might as well become good friends, huh?

DEFINE: Ideal

A person or thing regarded as perfect; a standard of beauty, perfection, or excellence; existing only in the imagination—desirable or perfect, but not likely to become a reality

---

Now, why do I call it a body love "battle"? Well, because our culture clings to an "ideal" of beauty, with some minor variations, and therefore we must always (or almost always) be in reaction to, if not direct warfare with, that ideal. Each of the teen girls in my workshops can easily describe this "ideal": skinny, big boobs and a not-too-big butt, long legs, tall, no stretch marks, toned, tan, big eyes, small nose, skinny, skinny, skinny, and then more skinny. Even if we don't believe that this "ideal" is ideal (and most of us sitting in the circle don't), we can all describe it, because it is everywhere—magazines, store windows, TV shows, movies, music videos, fashion runways, high school hallways, and on and on and on.

For now, let's not judge it; let's just look at it and acknowledge that it exists as a part of our daily lives. This "ideal" may be something we strive to achieve or strive to ignore. Its existence may torture us, or we may feel totally indifferent to it (there aren't many in that latter group, I'm willing to bet). But somewhere in your life, even if it doesn't affect you, there is a girl out there—a friend, a sister, a classmate, or a fellow teammate—trying, trying, *trying* to reconcile this "ideal" with her absolutely real body. I am nineteen years old. The years between fourteen and eighteen were *rough* for me as far as "exuberant" body love goes. At age sixteen, I was probably at an all-time low. I obsessed; I broke my body down into pieces that I "liked" and "didn't like" (or even hated sometimes); I soaked myself in guilt after eating an apple out of boredom instead of hunger; and, sometimes, quietly, following the lead of a new group of high school girls, I skipped lunch (even though my stomach was growling). My body was a nagging and constant focus for me. And that is why I write this chapter, with all my heart, for you—because sometimes, the whole body issue can be kind of overwhelming, no matter how strong we are.

Every single society, from cavewoman times to the modern day, has an ideal of beauty—a collective vision of what is the most *desirable*. And even if everyone doesn't agree on this "ideal," they can at least put a name—and usually a face—to it. And most of us have experienced some pressure to conform to this particular physical type.

Do you agree with the description of our current society's ideal of beauty that I laid out before? Is there an ideal in your home? In your community? In your school? Are they all the same? Sometimes they are, but sometimes they aren't.

Have you ever experienced pressure to look like this ideal? Sometimes the pressure takes the form of a super-direct comment (like a kindly meant remark from a relative, friend, coach, or the like, or maybe a not-so-kindly one). Other times it's more subtle (just a feeling, one that you may not even fully admit to yourself, that you *know* you won't be liked or attractive if you don't look this ONE way). I know I have experienced this—often despite my best intentions! I didn't *want* to judge parts of my body, but sometimes I got carried away by the "ideal" around me.

Historical ideals of beauty have always been based, under the surface at least, on very basic things, such as the amount of food available to a population. For example, in societies with food shortages, the plumpest and curviest are often considered to be the most attractive, because the extra weight shows that you have the money and time to eat. In societies with a *ton* of food (ours, for example), the opposite tends to be true: those with the time and the means to stay skinny (belong to a gym, work out, buy premade nutritious meals, and so on) prove their status, sometimes unconsciously, through their skinny, toned bodies. The shape or state of our bodies is often used to "prove" social status or membership in a certain class or group. Hmm, does this ring a bell, anyone? Certain high schools or middle schools maybe?

Not only has every single society throughout history had an ideal version of beauty, but also *most of these ideals have been different.* Many of these ideals seem just *ridiculous* to us today. For example, the ancient Aztecs are said to have prized those individuals with pointed heads, pointed teeth, and crossed eyes. With this goal in mind, they would tie boards to their babies' heads (hoping to mold the soft skull into a more angular shape), dangle objects before their babies' noses (hoping to increase those *attractive* cross-eyed tendencies), and regularly file their teeth (fierce!).

Or perhaps you have heard about the ancient Chinese practice of foot binding? This ideal of miniature-footed beauty originated around the year 937 CE and continued well into the 1900s. Upperclass girls had their feet systematically broken and bound between the ages of two and five to stunt their growth. As a result, most, if not *all*, of these women were never able to walk beyond extremely short distances (like from one room to another). Instead, they had to be carried, which showed their status. After all, peasant women would never have the luxury of being carried. They had to work, so their feet were left unbound. Ah, beauty!

Another example of binding for beauty took place in Victorian England in the form of those infamous corsets. At the onset of puberty, young women would bind their waists with whalebone or metal-stiff corsets in an effort to reach the "ideal" hourglass shape. Ahem, the only problem?

1. We have ribs, and bound ribs will not grow normally.

2. We have lungs, and bound lungs can't breathe normally. Hence all the talk of dainty ladies fainting. How *feminine*. And of course, *good* girls wore their corsets to bed, too. What a nightmare!

Around eleventh grade, I had a life-changing, norm-shattering epiphany: simply put, *I realized that I should have been born in Renaissance Italy.* Let me explain. In that time and in that place, I would have been just *gorgeous.* I am, quite frankly, *meant* to be in a painting by the Italian painter Botticelli—specifically, his painting of Venus stepping from the waves on the huge half-shell of an oyster. Have you ever seen those white soft curvy thighs of hers, without tone or tan? I've got 'em. The soft lower belly curve? Mine. The rather flat, but wide, large, white butt? Yup, mine too. And the flowing brown hair? All mine! Gosh, back *there* and *then,* I would have been a real STUNNER.

So answer this question for me: Where and when should you have been born? Because here's the crazy, fantastic fact about the relativity of ideal beauty: *we all have a place and/or a time where our bodies, just the way they are, would have been the absolute ideal of beauty.* We just happen to have been born in this time and in this place, today. Now I do love our modern age. Let's be real, it's BY FAR the best time—perhaps ever in history—to be a woman. In Renaissance Italy, the most I could have hoped for was to be a rich, semieducated, disempowered piece of eye candy for a rich man. Not my idea of a good time. But it's a *fascinating*, perspective-changing idea: *beauty truly is relative.*

My learning about the history of ideal beauty in other cultures has given me some much-needed perspective about beauty and desirability, and I hope it gives you the same. Can't we just go ahead and label ourselves—and definitely our society—as being just as ridiculous and cruel as the foot binders, corset tighteners, and tooth filers of history? I think that our society's virtually unobtainable ideals are "binding" us girls (look like this, don't eat that, fit into that size) and that we *do* have a choice to be free of these constraints. There is no *one* kind of beauty. No two people look exactly the same (not even identical twins—their unique walks and gestures shape their physical being as well). Each of us is unique (cheesy perhaps, but *true*). Your body, your walk, your mannerisms—they're all *yours,* so ROCK them. And worrying about "fat" may not be the best use of our energy, anyway.

DEFINE: Fat

(1) noun
A vital kind of body tissue (and cell) that serves as a source of energy.
It allows for the female hormone estrogen to be produced and
for a teenage girl to develop in puberty and get her period; it also
cushions and insulates vital organs. Also known as adipose tissue.

DEFINE: Fat

(2) noun
One of the six categories of **nutrients** found in food that the body needs
in order to function normally. Healthy fats include unsaturated omega-3s
and omega-8s. Fat is a part of any nutritionally complete meal.

DEFINE: Fat

(3) adjective
1. Fat as a body characteristic: Having a large amount of adipose tissue.
Plump, well fed.
2. Fat as a feeling: an all-inclusive, self-descriptive word, meaning
unhappy, guilty, unattractive, undesirable, or something
similarly negative. As in, "I feel so fat."
3. Fat as a personality trait: Meaning lazy, dumb, unmotivated,
mean, always hungry, never attractive, slow, nonathletic, and so on.
As in, "Well, there are the popular girls, the smart girls,
the funny hippie chicks, and the fat girls."

Fat, Fat, Fat. Say it out loud. Yes. Right now. I mean it. Why? Because F-A-T (three simple letters) has become a *dirty* word in our society. It's like a curse or an insult that can never be taken back. "Who would *ever* want to be called fat?" asks the shaming voice of our skinny-obsessed culture.

My childhood babysitter, Lisa, was over three hundred pounds. She was a big lady, and, yes, she was *fat*. When I was little, she took care of me and my neighbor Wiley. Our favorite game when we were about five was Big Rock, where Wiley and I played frolicking, barking seals sliding down our warm, friendly rock: Lisa. She was the model for me of accepting and loving her natural size. One time, a few years later, Lisa was out shopping at our local grocery store, and in the same aisle was a four-year-old girl and her mother. The little girl stared up in unmasked shock and awe (as kids will do) at Lisa's size. Abruptly she gasped, "Mommy, that woman is *really, really FAT!!*" Her mother was mortified. "Oh, I'm so, *so* sorry, she doesn't know what she's saying," she gasped. Lisa graciously turned to them, all three hundred–plus pounds of her, and smiled. "Oh, it's okay," she said, "I *am* fat." And then she moved on to the next aisle.

What if we could all be that cool, calm, and collected, that at peace with our natural body size? And I say *natural* because, yes, some people are, by birth and by genes, larger than others. There seems to be a cultural misperception that anyone above a certain weight or clothing size *must* be unhealthy and nonathletic. But that is not true! My aunt—lovely curvy lady that she is (and a softball player in her local women's league)—uses the phrase "fit and fat." The two terms aren't mutually exclusive.

There is a movement in the United States that calls "size-ism" the last socially acceptable prejudice in our culture. Beyond the nasty fat humor and fat insults that we've all heard, there are actual statistics that speak to prejudice on a wider scale within the workplace and even the schoolyard. One study shows that when elementary school children are shown a picture of a kid in a wheelchair and a fat kid, they would prefer to be friends with the disabled kid. That's illuminating.

So what can we do?

1. Let's reclaim the word *fat* and say what we actually mean rather than using the word as a catchall for anything negative. Fat is not an emotion or a way of skipping the process of discovering what you *really* feel. If you hear yourself bemoaning the fact that you "feel fat," push yourself to identify your true feeling instead. Or maybe it is a friend or family member who needs this extra push. Is it "unattractive" that you feel? Or "bloated"? Or "unhappy"? Or "frustrated"? What do you "feel fat" about? Then with your emotional intelligence, you can begin to deal with that *true* feeling.

2. Call people out when they use the word *fat* in a way that you find offensive. You don't have to do it aggressively. In fact, you can be quite polite, because people are often unaware of what they're saying. Maybe they meant to be insulting, or maybe they didn't. Either way, you can say something. Consider other words that make you uncomfortable when used negatively.

3. Use the word *fat* kindly and considerately regarding yourself. The battle starts with us, every day, in the mirror or listening to the chatter of the voice in our heads. If you find yourself judging yourself because of your weight or shape, try the following:

   a. Name three things that you *love* about your body. Write them down. Memorize them. Repeat them to yourself when you find yourself getting judgmental.

   b. Like I've learned to do (wacky, but it works), simply kiss your palm, gently pat the area of your body that you're judging, and whisper: "Good thigh. I'm sorry I was mean. You don't deserve it. I love you." Challenge yourself every single day to be more compassionate to yourself (and not just about "fat"). Be as kind to yourself as you would be to your best friend.

DEFINE: Estrogen

A hormone, produced and stored in the ovaries, that creates and sustains the developments of the female characteristics of the body, including the cycle of menstruation; mainly found in females, but also present in much smaller quantities in males (and vice versa with testosterone, the male hormone that is also found in small quantities in females); high amounts are found in women between menarche (first period) and the end of menopause (last period)

This is the body-truth section. Here you will find short truths to snap up quickly, repeat loudly to anyone who will listen, and remember for yourself forever.

The first body truth is that each and every body has natural cycles of change: it shifts its shape, weight, boob size, thigh size, belly size, hair color, skin texture, monthly periods, and so on.

These cycles should be expected. There are two categories of cycles: life cycles and seasonal cycles.

Life cycles are puberty, periods, pregnancy, menopause, and the like. They happen to every woman. Physically, there are many consistent and somewhat predictable developments in each one of our cycles. Our emotional and intellectual responses to the changes these cycles bring can be quite different. One of my favorite stories about puberty involves my mom's friend Caroline, who works as a health coach. She has one daughter, Julia, who's a few years older than I am and who has long black hair, a wide smile, and a passion for reading fantasy books (a passion that I quickly picked up). When Julia was about thirteen, she started to put weight onto her girl's body, and it wasn't just a butt or boobs (which she was kind of expecting). She began to have love handles and some padding on her belly and thighs.

One day, passing the mirror in her bedroom, it struck her. "MOMMMMM!!!!" she called, "I'VE GOT FAT!!!!!" I think Caroline did the best thing a mom could ever do. She jumped up from her desk in the kitchen and rushed to her daughter's room to celebrate. "Oooohhh, where??" she responded. "Honey, that's so exciting, FAT??!! Show me!!" She then proceeded to explain to Julia that fat meant her body was getting ready to become a woman's body, and that it's natural for some girls to find more fat on their bodies just before they develop boobs and get taller and get their periods. So finding a little extra fat was 100 percent natural and, as a sign of things to come, a cause for celebration.

In fact, if a teen girl's body were not to put on this healthy weight, it would not be able to give the girl her period. The body needs these stores of fat to make the hormone estrogen, which is responsible for changing a girl's body into a woman's body. Unfortunately, many people misunderstand the body's natural life cycles and mistake them for a sign of some kind of "pending obesity" or problem behavior on the part of the girl. But this is often wrong! So, now you know. Let's reassess (dispose of, get rid of, BANISH) our culture's ridiculous "ideal" and help young girls find their body confidence.

Seasonal cycles are the way your body naturally changes and shifts throughout the ups and downs, colds and hots of one year. I have found that my body often changes in a predictable pattern season by season. In winter, like any smart animal preparing for the cold, I'm apt to gain a little bit of weight: fat to keep me warm. My mom has often reminded me (and I mean *often*) the story of how when I was fourteen, I was lying on the couch one March evening and spontaneously started patting my belly. "Hello, winter belly," I said matter-of-factly. "I'll be coming out of hibernation soon, and then we'll have to say good-bye." In summer, I often lose a little weight, even without trying: I sweat more, lose some of my normal winter appetite in the heat, and am more outdoorsy and active. Trust your body. It is smart. You can notice these cycles, accept them, and celebrate your body's intelligence.

DEFINE: Set Point

The natural, genetic, healthy weight range that your body tries to maintain; a balance of intake and output that your body seeks (often despite your hardest efforts to gain or lose weight through diet or exercise change)

The second body truth is the simple fact that we all have what's called a *set point*. And this number (or range of numbers) is determined by our inherited, unchangeable genes, and not by how many hours we spend on an exercise machine. Our body finds its natural shape and "happy place" when we are eating healthfully and being active (yes, the "being active" part counts!) in our daily lifestyle.

What if the goal for body love were body *trust?* Trust that your body is *smart,* that it has its own kind of intuition. Trust that if you feed your body what it needs and keep it active, it will find its natural biological set point—and, after that, perhaps your job is just to accept it? Accept the shape you're in, because the fact is, it's going to be your body for the rest of your life. It's time to take a deep breath and release yourself from any sort of body guilt or obsession. There's no changing YOU, so now your job is to *love* you. And *you* includes your body.

DEFINE: Diet

The kinds of foods that a person, animal, or community habitually eats; for example, "Anteaters have a normal diet of ants," or "Eliza's average diet consists of dark chocolate, Earl Grey tea with milk and honey, hamburgers, zucchini, and maple custard"

Or . . .

A special course of food that a person restricts to in order to lose weight or for medical reasons; for example, "Barbara only ate carrots for a month. She started to turn slightly orange," or "Chrisso was lactose intolerant so he avoided most dairy products and drank soy milk instead of cow's milk"

The third body truth is about diets, and it is simple: despite the myth that diets work, they just plain don't. Yes, despite the testimonials and the never-ending magazine articles proclaiming a "miracle cure," *diets don't work* as a way to keep weight off permanently. The fact is that 95 percent of all dieters will regain the weight they have lost, and often more than that, within one to five years. Although "starvation techniques" might "work" in the short term, they are never sustainable and do not contribute to a healthy lifestyle or a healthy relationship with your body. By the law of human bodies, your diet will always "fail," and you are likely to end up feeling like a "failure." Instead, invest your energy in a little bit of self-love.

Geneen Roth, a brilliant author and teacher on this subject of why diets don't work, says that "the fourth law of the universe is that for every diet there is an equal and opposite binge." I think she understands physics pretty darn well—in my experience, whenever I skip meals or restrict food, I have always ended up overeating (what Geneen calls a "binge") as a result. When we don't eat regular meals and snacks, our blood sugar takes a dive and we can become desperately hungry and then desperately overeat! So throw away your diets! THEY DON'T WORK!

DEFINE: Metabolism

The process and rate through which your body turns food into fuel; influenced by age, sex, amount of muscle mass, and your genetics

The fourth body truth is that when we think about bodies, we often think about *food:* what we're going to eat, when we're going to eat it, and how much, *exactly,* is going to pass through our lips. Our culture's obsession with body shape, size, and weight goes hand in glorious hand with our culture's obsession with *food, food, food!* I love food. I especially love good food. There have been many times when I have eaten out of boredom, a handful of times when I have eaten out of sadness, and, as I said in the beginning of the chapter, even a few times when I lost my center and tried to stop eating certain meals altogether in order to "get skinny." When you skip meals, your body begins to go into starvation mode; it thinks you are entering a famine, a time where there is simply not enough food to go around. And so to protect you and to prolong its ability to function, your body slows down your *metabolism,* or the rate at which your body processes food. You are actually more likely to gain weight when you skip meals, which is exactly what happened to me. Eating regular meals is the best plan for having a healthy, strong, well-fueled body and for your metabolism to work most efficiently. It's simple science. Spread the word. (Some girls *really* need to hear this one.)

DEFINE: Scale

1. A standardized system of value judgments used to measure something
2. A mechanism (sometimes a torture device) used to check weight change and to measure against "average" or "ideal."
In certain cases, it serves as a gauge for how we approach the day:
Am I skinny and happy today? Or fat and sad?

We can hardly talk about bodies without talking about our moms. In chapter 2, we opened up the reality of *emotional inheritance,* a new level of understanding and choice about the way we communicate, relate, and cry/yell/lock it all up inside now that we have entered the teen years. But now it's time to talk about *physical inheritance.* As ever, it's part fate, part destiny. I want to ask the big question: What can we do to *daughter* our moms around the hot topic of bodies?

Now we do not, of course, inherit our *entire* attitude toward our body from just our mom, but let's face the facts: *the way our mom deals with her body and food has a huge impact on the way we deal with our body and food.* Thus, just as with our emotional inheritance, we also have our physical inheritance to understand, accept, work with, love, and celebrate.

The way I see it, there are two things on the spectrum of physical inheritance that we teenage girls get from our moms:

1. **Our physical body shape and size (from our biological mom).** On the body *shape* side of things, I do not have my mom's legs or her breasts or her eyes (they're my gram's, on my dad's side), but I do have her hair, her hands, her toes, and her hips. I have my dad's nose, blue eyes, scraggly eyebrows, and high-set waist. These are facts to acknowledge, accept, and laugh about. If you were adopted, then there are often more differences than similarities to share, understand, and celebrate.

2. **Our relationship with our body and food (from the mom who raised us).** Sometimes your mom's feelings about her body and food may take the form of dieting, or sometimes they may pour themselves into a stream of seemingly endless negative comments about her body (or someone else's body—a spouse's? a friend's? maybe yours?). A mom who breaks her body down into pieces that she "likes" and "doesn't like" ("I just hate my thighs, they're so HUGE") will likely have a daughter who does the same. A mom who fears her own aging and idealizes her daughter's youth (a beautiful thing, but not the *only* beauty in this world) will likely have a daughter who, later in life, will find it hard to see beauty in her wrinkles and graying hair. And the mom who accepts her body's shape (and its changes) with acceptance, grace, and humor will model this for her daughter. A mom who loves her own body will be able to help her daughter truly love *her* own body.

Rebecca was a friend in my freshman year of college, a slender, curvy-calved, red-haired science geek. She was image focused—constantly pulling her black shirt down over her waist and self-consciously tugging her silver sparkly skirt this way or that. She was brave, though. She dove right into talking about the whole body-image thing on our first dinner together. She did not doubt where her fault-finding relationship with her body came from. "My mom *hates* her body," she said. "She's always looking for one way to lose weight or another: jeans that 'burn fat' or a new exercise plan. She never stops talking about it." Does she say things about your body, too? I asked. "Nope, here's the thing: she makes a point of telling me every day how *beautiful* I am, how perfect, how I could *never* think anything bad about myself. And I want to *scream* at her, 'MOM, I AM YOU!!! How can you be ugly and I be beautiful?!'" Rebecca hit the table for emphasis. "It just makes me so *sad*. I want her to love herself. And I want to be able to love *my*self." Just that realization, that vision up the matriline, is a feat of *daughtering*. The question is whether she can take it home with her and whether her mom would be ready to listen.

There are endless stories about moms and food. Don't believe me? Just ask one of your friends. My friend Elsie, a spiky-blonde-haired girl who I met at summer camp when I was eleven, said that in her family, the females "eat their emotions together," like a family ritual or tradition. "I mean, we would sit with my mom in front of the TV, snacking and snacking and *snacking,* especially when she was stressed or sad or pissed off. We'd all do it together, my mom and my little sister and me. It was like a comfort thing." It was only as Elsie turned seventeen that she started to become aware of the pattern, and now, as she turns twenty-one, she has stopped eating when she isn't hungry. Who knows? Maybe her mom will never change—or maybe she will (that would be some *daughtering* feat)—but at least Elsie is aware of the problem and has begun to make her own changes.

My friend Rachel's mom, Susan, taught her how to diet when she was twelve and was putting on "baby fat" (that means, ahem, she was about to get her period, as *you* now understand). Susan genuinely believed she was performing an act of kindness, not a misinformed intervention; she thought she was doing her daughter a favor, as if the *art of dieting* were some kind of sacred female tradition to be passed on from mother to daughter under the light of a full moon.

My friend Karen, tall and self-confident with big curly hair, inherited a positive body image from her mom. Her mom had a direct, no-nonsense approach to Karen's relationship with her body: absolute love of its strengths and imperfections was a requirement. One lunch period in eighth grade, Karen reached into her backpack and passed this love poem to me. It was called "Thunder Thighs," and, as the story goes, it had been written with affection to her twenty-year-old mom by a boyfriend who took a phrase that was usually insulting and turned it into a love ode to his girlfriend's beautiful thighs. Karen chuckled at my expression of amazement ("Who the HECK wrote this? This is GREAT!") and jokingly slapped her own thighs. "Look at these strong babies. Yup, they're *inherited*."

Even though I've struggled some with my own body image, ultimately, I inherited a positive body image from my mom. Because she worked hard to heal her negative body image before I was even born, I grew up in a house with no scales, and I was fully aware that my mom was happy living in her curvaceous body. But it is never, *never* too late for a mom to heal her body image, even if she is the mom of a teenage daughter! And, yes, YOU can be the one to push her in that direction. This is an example of *daughtering*: the active role that a teen daughter can begin to play in her relationship with her mom.

Consider sharing your favorite realizations from this body chapter with your mom.

Body Guidelines

I have come to realize that a negative inner dialogue about my body is a *brain drain* on my time. Courtney Martin, the fabulous twenty-five-year-old author of *Perfect Girls, Starving Daughters*, estimates that women spend an average of a hundred minutes a day "scrutinizing instead of loving their bodies."[5] When you hear your inner body critic click on, *just turn it off* (say to it, "I'm not going there today!"), and re-channel those one hundred minutes into something that makes you happy or that gives you a sense of purpose.

Here is a list of things that you can do every day to move closer to body love, body trust, and body acceptance:

1. **Notice and dismiss the small judgmental voice in your head.** "Perfect" does not exist. Seek realness, acceptance, confidence, humor, and love instead. Write down at least three things you love about your body. Repeat them to yourself when you hear that judgmental voice.

2. **Throw out your scale.** A number in the morning shouldn't have the power to determine how your day goes. Other viable (and preferable) options for a morning check-in include asking yourself: How do I *feel* this morning? What am I looking forward to today? What am I not so excited about today? How did I sleep? And so on and so forth. If someone has the audacity to ask you what you weigh, smile and answer, "I have no idea."

3. **Cut out the size label in your clothes.** Don't judge your body by the P, S, M, L, or XL tag that you find in your clothes or by a number size, either. Sizing varies from company to company, and size ZERO is an insult to our real bodies. Make sure your clothes are comfortable.

4. **Do not diet.** Period. End of story.

5. **Do not count calories.** The knowledge of what your body needs is not in an external scale (unless, of course, you have a medical condition that requires a special diet!), but in an internal one: be body smart. Seek out foods that make you feel energetic and revived, even hours after you've eaten them, instead of foods that make your energy crash just twenty minutes later. Always go for balance: veggies, protein, fats, and carbohydrates make up a balanced meal or snack.

6. **Eat when you're hungry and stop when your body has had enough.** These are two of Geneen Roth's seven eating practices that can be found in her fantastic books, which my mom and I both love.[6] It's the most natural thing in the world to listen to your body's cues, but somehow we seem to forget it once we leave wise babyhood behind. Eating should be a natural process, a daily cycle of listening to your body.

7. **Find body-image role models who are older than you.** Maybe it's your mom, an aunt, or a friend's mother, or maybe it's an older girl or a public figure. Someone who accepts and loves her body.

DEFINE: Sexuality

A person's sexual orientation or preference (who and what they are attracted to), a capacity for sexual feelings, or sexual activity

---

When we begin to talk about teenage girls and bodies, we invite, metaphorically speaking, a giant elephant into the room. Elephants aren't all that subtle, especially in the middle of my little writing room, so there's absolutely no ignoring it, ladies: SEX. Yes, that's right, I want to talk about sex, sexuality, being sexy, and the nearly universal reality of desire. Our sexuality—the thoughts we may or may not have, the actions we may or may not take—is a huge part of who we authentically ARE as teenage girls. Not only that, but the rest of the world seems pretty keen on—nigh on obsessed with— our sexuality or our "pure and virginal" lack of it. If we aren't talking about it, well, then I think we may be the only ones.

I believe that, in general, we, as a culture, don't *really* talk about sex and sexuality—unless it's a rude joke or about a man, and he's usually having lots of it or none of it. Funny! *Real* talk about what it means to mix sex and love or to have someone other than you touch your body (and to want them to or not want them to) is rarely, if ever, discussed. But I think we desperately *need* to talk about it in an honest, open, and thoughtful way. Sexuality—specifically when it concerns us teenage girls—has become so complex and convoluted in pop culture, and so powerful and polarizing in the teen-girl world, that it certainly needs some sorting out. Frankly, I believe that it's when we don't talk about sexuality that we get in the most trouble.

Now some moms, I am sure, would prefer it if I didn't talk about sex at all ("Oh, my daughter doesn't do those things. She isn't thinking about *those things* yet."). As I said before, I believe some moms are simply *afraid* of the intensity of love and sexuality, the new roller coaster that will take their child daughter further from emotional "safety." And gosh, what a scary thing (for me almost as much as my mom)! But let me promise you one thing—whether you're my girl reader or a mom anxiously scanning this over her shoulder—girl teenagers *are* thinking about sex, sexuality, and desire. You, girl reader, know that. Duh. It may seem silly, obvious, or embarrassing to admit, but my point is, it shouldn't be. I don't mean that you're necessarily having sex yourself (though you probably know someone who is), but it *does* cross your mind. It's a fascination and a feeling. There's something mysterious, maturely "intense," exciting, and kind of *scary* about it all. At least that was how I felt. So let's find an open conversation and a true form of our sexuality that's worth celebrating. And what more perfect place than in the Body Trust chapter? Sexuality (though it is a new conversation for us) is connected to the vital topics of our earlier chapters: intuition and emotional intelligence. Our truest guide in discovering, exploring, and understanding our sexual selves is, as ever, that voice in our gut: our REAL self. So, first and foremost, we must learn and remember to listen to ourselves.

I believe that the concept of sexuality—a real girl's sexuality—has been hijacked and transformed into a sellable product, something that belongs to everyone *but* its true owner: YOU, ME, us teenage girls. Sexuality has become part of a stereotype; it's what "bad girls" do and "good girls" don't do, instead of being a natural part of a whole person's identity or an act of love. It's the line drawn between the stereotype of the "slut" and the "virgin" or the "whore" and the "prude"—you pick one, there are endless names for it. And all too often, it's a trap that we teenage girls fall into: How do we define ourselves? How do we define others in relation to our sexuality? I want us—yes, you and me here reading this book, and all of us teenage girls—to reimagine sex as part of our whole identity that we can be comfortable discovering; to imagine choosing *what* we want and *when* we want it *when* our mind, heart, and body are ready. Let's get over the fuss and the embarrassment; sex is something that (almost) all girls want at some point in their lives (and, yes, there are some people who are just not really that sexual or, as it is commonly called, "asexual"). As with "big red ideas," let's get rid of the awkward mystery and get comfortable.

As I entered into the teen years, I found that the first way my identity began to mix with sexuality was not in a literal act but in a new idea, expectation, and desire to *be sexy*. Perhaps you are feeling something similar. As our bodies develop from less girl to more woman, and our brains and teen hormones catch up, sexuality can become a way to get attention. For some it is the norm of their middle or high school: push-up bras, thongs, and crop tops are the new language of "popularity." Are you *hot*? Are you *wanted*? The mere idea of sex—being "sexy"—can often become a new form of girl power. And each social group, school, or community can have its own way of communicating this—sometimes it's a casual code, sometimes a blatant statement.

I love feeling sexy. It's exciting—the way a thrill goes through my whole body when I feel *wanted,* when I haven't been wanted like that before. But my sexiness is one piece, and just one piece, of who I am as a person, a girlfriend, a lover, and, one day, I believe, a life partner. I am also intellectual, enthusiastic, *rather* witty, loyal, and snuggly (among other things). Speaking personally, to be treated as a sexual object, without my other qualities attached, makes me rather nauseous. The way I present myself often dictates the attention I receive: sometimes I wear soft baggy sweaters and knee-high boots, and other times a slinky mini. Sometimes I like the attention of a complimentary look or comment, and sometimes I want to curse them out for staring. Either way, I know it's MY sexiness, my body, and my identity, and I also know I'm a whole lot more than all that. **And I have the power to decide when someone gets to touch me or not.**

Think about, for example, the self that you put out on the Internet. In our day and age, the Internet is most often the entry ground for sexuality (cue the Facebook check), for proving our "sexiness" and "desirability," and for beginning the flirtations that can lead to literal sex and sexual exploration. Some social scientists call our Internet personality a "second self" (another version of ourselves that we have to take care of, check up on, make sure looks good every day). How do you want to present this second self? How do you want to be seen? What kind of attention do you want? What attention don't you want? The truth is this: outside of the absurd "norms" of the teen world (be sure to seek out new "norms" if those ones are getting you down), you are the only one who gets to make the choice of how you present yourself and who you aim to be and become. Listen to your gut, your intuition, and your real intelligence as you think about these questions: What are *my* values? Who am *I*? Be conscious of how you truly want to present yourself—this is an identity *choice*. Make it count.

Now, for the sake of clarity, when I speak about "sexuality" or "sex," I do not intend to necessarily speak about one specific act or another, nor am I referring to some code of "bases." In my opinion, sex and "virginity" are what *you* define them as; it's all a personal matter. All of sex and sexuality can be intense, intimate, pleasurable, and confusing. It can make you nauseous if done in a situation or with a person who makes you feel uncomfortable—or worse, violated. Speaking personally, I can honestly say that earlier "stages" of sex—foreplay and the like—were more intense and identity shaking than the later, more classically "intimate" acts that came when I was older and, honestly, more ready to cope with the intensity of them. But that has just been my experience, and it may not be yours.

The flipside of the fun, joy, and pleasure of sex is unfortunately the pain, confusion, guilt, and violation that comes when boundaries are crossed and in sexual assault and rape. When sex is not *consensual*—meaning when both people don't want to be part of any type of sexual activity (whether it's foreplay or intercourse) and are not saying an enthusiastic "YES!" with their words, face, *and* body—then we have entered into violation. At my college, there is a sex-education week, and for the one day highlighting the dangers of sexual assault and rape, the campus is filled with students in hot-pink tee shirts reading this important message: CONSENSUAL SEX IS HOT. Let's say that loud and proud and take the scary conversation of assault or violation out of the shadows: we teenage girls will only accept a sex and sexuality that *we*, and the other person, *want* with our *whole* bodies and beings.

It is important to reframe sexual assault or rape not as something that just happens to "other people"; it touches one in three women worldwide, regardless of socioeconomic status, age, heritage, or skin color. We will all know someone in our lifetime who has been sexually assaulted or raped. If it doesn't touch our own bodies—and I pray that it doesn't—it will touch the lives of those close to us. I think that very often people hesitate to define an action or a situation as "sexual assault" or "rape" because of the extremity of those terms; it sounds like such a drastic accusation! But sexual assault and rape are real, and they are drastic, and when boundaries are crossed—the boundaries of our bodies, and the power we have to choose—we must be awake. If something has happened to you or to a friend, speak about it. Find someone you trust—specifically, an adult you trust—and SPEAK. SPEAK until you are sure you have been heard. SPEAK until you have said everything. This is not something that anyone asks for, should ever feel guilty for having had happen to them, or should ever have to carry alone.

Sexuality, our sexuality, is something we can live and claim—or perhaps reclaim, if we need to—for ourselves as part of our core identity. If sex and sexuality are looming on the horizon or are the heat and intensity of your current life, then here are my thoughts: I hope that my words here are a beginning, or a helpful addition, to a lifelong conversation with yourself about sexuality. Remember, information is power, and useful information is at your fingertips—on the Internet, in books, in people. Go read, ask, discover, reflect. Find the books that answer the questions you're asking and the people who can open up these oh-so-human conversations with you.

Important Stuff About Sexuality

1. Any "stage" of sex is intense. The physical actions inspired by desire, intimacy, lust, and love are accompanied by brain changes: neurons fire through new pathways in the brain, releasing powerful rushes of emotion and, often, pleasure. Evolutionarily speaking, our brains are wired to understand sexual activity as a "mating for life." In prehistoric times, it was in our best survival interest to pair off for life, for the support that a mated "partner" could provide in raising the next generation. So, translating that to modern times, however honest someone's intention may be to make a physical act "casual," the brain's neurons, emotional patterns, hormones, endorphins, and so on will *always* be conspiring in the opposite direction. From the perspective of the brain and emotional-health professionals, immediate or easy detachment after such intimacy is really hard to do. So, step back and grasp the whole picture. Bottom line: sex is intense. It's a game changer for any relationship and for any person.

2. Any kind of sex is supposed to be pleasurable. If you're *not* enjoying it, ask yourself this oh-so-important question: *Why* are you having it? News flash: we are no longer in the prehistoric age (whew), and so sexual activity for the sole sake of creating the next generation (and the survival of your genes!) has lost much of its urgency. Instead, we've found another reason. Sex is (mostly) about *pleasure* and *love*. The same question applies to the "earlier bases" of sex: ask yourself *why*? In my heart of hearts, I believe that sex is not—and should not be—for popularity, power, or image. Sex is not a way to be liked or to just avoid having to say "no." Sex is for you.

3. Get smart about sex: BE SAFE. Sex may be fun, and sometimes funny, but getting pregnant when you're not ready isn't, nor is getting an STI (sexually transmitted infection). Good information is available online, in books, and from experts in person. But make sure you trust your source, rather than the rumor mill, however well-intentioned your "knowing" friend may be.

4. It's time to learn how to speak about our bodies, including and especially the parts of our bodies attached to our sexuality. We live in a time of vagina-revolution: Eve Ensler's *Vagina Monologues* has spread like wildfire to college campuses around the world, and, just a few months before this writing, an online storm came to the rescue of a woman legislator in the Ohio state senate who was censored for speaking the word "vagina" in her comments on a law on women's health.

5. Here's the big truth—let this one sink down in deep—at the heart of sex and sexuality should be *communication*, *trust*, and *self-trust* (or your intuition). If you are body smart (a type of our many intelligences!), you know what you want and when you feel safe. LISTEN to your body.

So listen to this. Really listen, because I have one last realization to drop on your most open self: What if you saw your body as *special,* as something that was even sacred? It is *yours* (and only yours), and as Eve Ensler, an activist for girls and women, said in her book *I Am an Emotional Creature: The Secret Life of Girls Around the World:* "No one will know your body better than you." Love it. Hold it when it needs holding (yes, sometimes you don't need someone else to make you feel better). Give it massages, good rest, good food, and activity. Dance it across the kitchen, down the street, and into the waves. Chase the ecstasy of movement that expresses your emotion and strength in the rippling of your muscles that connect you to your core. Give your body hot tea with honey when it's sore, Epsom salt baths when it's achy, and layers and layers of soft clothes when it's grumpy and cold. And when it's feeling especially celebrational, deck it in your favorite clothes (Bright pink underwear that no one else knows about but you? Your favorite scarf? Those trusty jeans?). You've only got one body, and it's worth pampering, celebrating, respecting, and gosh, *enjoying.*

5

Girl Trust

....

*No person is your friend who demands your
silence, or denies your right to grow.*
—ALICE WALKER

AS SOON AS THE TWENTY or so daughters gather alone with me at our Mothering & Daughtering workshops, the babble of conversation begins, and most of the stories shared and questions asked are about friendship. How do you make it work when there are three best friends? Will someone always be left out? What do you do when "mean girls" are making your life miserable? When two of your close friends hate each other? Or when you realize your best friend is a "mean girl," and she brings out that side of you, too? What if you suddenly realize you have a crush on your best friend in the world? What if most of your close friends are older than you? Does that make your mom uncomfortable? How do you deal with not being ready for some of the stuff they might be doing? And what if your close friends are younger than you? Does that make you silly and immature? What if all of your friends are boys, or all girls? What do you *do?*

What I have found is that although no two people's experiences in the workshop are *exactly* alike, more often than not there are some eerie similarities—enough similarities that when we stop chattering and begin listening to each other, an attentive hush settles on the room. When Sally begins to talk about Alessandra and how, even though they've been best friends since kindergarten, she feels like she doesn't even know Alessandra anymore, like they've grown worlds apart in just the first year of high school, other hands sprout up around the circle, waving wildly for attention. "Me too, me too," the girls whisper to Sally. "That's just like me and my friend Netta." "That's like the *exact* story of what happened to me and Becca! That's crazy!" Though we are not the same, the common ground is undeniable, and we can't help grinning like fools when we realize that we are not alone. Not at all.

This chapter on girl trust is a response to the basic reality that the ups and downs of our everyday teen lives are oh-so-closely connected to what's going on in our most important friendships. Never before has our on-the-ground, day-to-day experience been so affected by what one close friend may say, do, or think. This new web of heart-to-heart, SMS-fed attachments—quite different from the playdates and the shifting alliances of our elementary school years—becomes, metaphorically speaking, the solar system in which we teens orbit. We just absolutely *have* to know: What did so-and-so say? What do you think of my new shirt? He likes *who*? What grade did you get? The very pulse of our lives can seem to come from the constellation of lovely friends we keep closest to us at any given time.

Unfortunately, the sun is not shining on all parts of our planet all of the time, and there is often a dark side of our friendships. Exaggerated though it may be, we teen girls do have a reputation for being *mean*. When it comes to the infamous corridors of middle-school friendship, we are the feared and featured poster girls, the sharks of the fish tank. No Hollywood teen movie or midlife mother's reflection on adolescence is complete without the image of the mean teen girl, in miniskirt and dark eye makeup (you know, how we supposedly *all* like to look). We inhabit a different kind of "war zone," where the rule is "All for none and none for all"! Our weapons are gossip, lies, catty looks, exclusive groups, expensive clothes, competition, and the appearance of perfection. It's survival of the fittest, *Lord of the Flies* rewritten for an all-girl cast and filmed on location right in your hometown.

But is this story we are told about middle school completely true? Are we powerless against the force this image has on our own expectations and self-image? And is living it out our only option? No, no, and no.

The reality is that we teenagers are trying out every kind of strategy we can find to figure out who we are, how to stay safe, and what is the best way to be close to someone our own age. Along the way, it can get rough. And so all the more reason for us—who each have the potential to channel our frustration or desperation for relationship into meanness—to arm our most genuine selves with the trusty tools we need to ride out this roller coaster safely.

So I ask you: *How do we ensure that we have the best, most genuine, and most fulfilling friendships possible?* Is there some kind of foolproof guidebook that we can learn by heart? Is there a trusty how-to manual for avoiding the pitfalls of changing allegiances and the bitterness of relationships left behind? Can we float on through to high school graduation like the kind, generous, luminous beings that we know we are in our heart of hearts, instead of slogging our way through the muddy slime that we may have heard middle school and even high school can be?

Well, dear girl reader, I'll be honest. No. There is likely no avoiding the first hurts that come with teenage friendship—ecstatic, giddy connection or the cold cut, right to the gut, of betrayal—or with teenage love (we've already talked about *that* in chapter 3). Life happens in cycles: day becomes night, winter becomes summer, and crappy days give way to gloriously sunny ones. There's no way around it. We are dead set on a collision course with overwhelming love, pain, sadness, and ecstasy. In fact, I pray that you do hit the road bumps that cause pain, because it is through them, through their very intensity (sobbing on the floor, jumping up and down on your bed, and so on) that you will learn about the true shape of your self. This can sometimes be a "dark night of the soul," if you choose to call it that. But if we are heart smart (chapter 3, again), we are pushed to grow to the next level of our full and truly adult potential.

All of this big new stuff does first show up in the hallways of middle school. In fact, the early teen years (and even some preteen ones) are the first time we begin to feel this "adult" intensity of emotion. The emotions experienced by a child are deep to be sure—have you ever heard a toddler wailing on the subway? But young children can't understand all the nuances of the situations around them, and so their emotional "reading" of any given situation is a bit fuzzy. They are protected from too much understanding.

But we teenagers are *not* protected from too much under-standing. Our new psychological perceptions of the larger world are pulsing through every cell of our body, burning through our brain's neural pathways for the very first time. We step into the teen years, push back the curtain on the adult drama, and suddenly we *get it* in a totally fresh way. Metaphorically speaking, we wake up. Scientifically speaking, this waking up is actually a new wiring of our brains. And it is *intense*.

Given this new intensity, there's all the more reason to make sure that someone has our back. What is trust, and why is it important?

DEFINE: Trust

A firm belief in the reliability, truth, ability, or strength of someone; often the same as "confidence" or "faith"

Trust is a word that has become so overused and bandied about among our generation that it is virtually meaningless. "Don't you trust me?" whispers my friend Jane across the aisle dividing our fifth-grade desks. Of course, I can hiss a quick "yes" in return, but I don't mean it, not really. All too often, from elementary school to middle school, "trust" has become synonymous with "friendship," and the secrets we share have become public badges of confidence in each other. However, as *we* grow older, our understanding of trust must grow up, too, or else we're likely to feel pretty lonely indeed.

A building has to have a strong base or else it will collapse during the first tremors of a storm. I see trust as that strong base, that vital *foundation* of every relationship we care about. For example, if there is no trust, how can you hope to open up to someone about how your day at school *really* was, or how scared you are about how you've begun to hate your "muffin top" hips, or how wacko, turn-bright-red, jaw-dropping in love you are with Miley? Without some kind of basic trust, our ability to be authentic with others—and maybe even with ourselves—is impaired, our ability to love is stymied, and our experience of living fully is halted. Instead we may end up nervous, forever watching our backs, and perhaps fundamentally ungrounded. It's an unhappy state.

So first of all, to me, trust is a feeling (*not* a brainy knowing) that rests inside your body, relaxing you. It comes from a confidence you *feel* that in that moment, with that friend, you can be whoever the heck you want to be—silly, thoughtful, guilty, depressed, giddy, or snuggly—and they get *you*. They haven't tried to fit you into a nice, neat little box. They *see* you, the whole perfectly imperfect you. To me, this is the ultimate safety and freedom, when you feel your whole body give a sigh of relief and relax into itself. It's the doll in your pocket whispering to you that you're safe. Do you know what I'm talking about?

Also vitally important is an understanding of how your *family* shows love and trust. You're a practiced "inheritance" detective by now, so you get just how key it is to see the models you were taught as a child, and you are likely now putting it into practice yourself (whether consciously or not). Do you trust your parents? Do you trust your siblings, if you have them? How do you earn trust? How do you establish it? I was lucky to have—and to *build*—a trusting relationship with my parents. It was something we both worked on—my mom to earn my trust, and I to earn hers. Without this layer, I feel that we are lost. What a scary place—to feel like we are constantly watching our back in this most fundamental of relationships.

As we leave behind the simple world of a child's sweet, automatic, and naive trust and enter the realm of teen friendships, we learn that trust is something that we can and must *build*. It truly requires *action* on our part. I have learned that trust is something I must work to build in my relationships. I have earned trust by not sharing the secret, by calling when I said I would, by answering a difficult question both honestly *and* kindly, by showing up as my heartfelt self when someone is sad, or by butting in when I see a friend heading down a dangerous path. I have also earned trust by making mistakes, owning them, and repairing what's broken. Once we reframe it like this, we can *choose* trust as something we need, deserve, and can give on the path forward to full-on authenticity.

DEFINE: Authenticity

Being real; being your truest, most genuine self without mask
or barrier between the individual and the outside world;
this can exist for just a moment or for the duration of an honest
conversation, or it can be the journey of a lifetime

When I was fifteen years old, I could easily define for you the different selves I presented to the world at large. I was the goof at dance class, the shy know-it-all at school, the "mother" of my neighborhood friends, and the smiling, helpful little girl at family holidays. We all have personae that we put on for different places in our lives. More often than not, we base these shifting selves on what we believe will make us feel *safe* in each of these different places. But I took it one step further. As you may understand, the many masks I wore were also created in reaction to specific people in my life. One friend got one version of Eliza, and another friend got a different version—in short, eager to please, I became the friend I thought each person most needed. I sometimes worried that if they compared notes, they would realize they were buddies with two completely different people. Today, even with my closest of friends, I still occasionally find myself wearing the mask of "Oh, I'm fine" instead of expressing my "At this moment I happen to be an emotionally vulnerable mess who just wants to curl up into a ball and cry" reality. I have found that masks can allow us to feel *safe*, but there's a price: nobody gets to see who you really are. And sometimes you can get so confused about the many masks you wear that you lose track of which one is *really* you. You may end up feeling like you've never had a chance to live fully as your genuine self. So you must ask important questions of yourself: "Do I really want to wear a mask at all? And if I do, do I have a choice about taking it off?"

We all—and specifically teenagers—live in a world of masks. These masks are not inherently bad; sometimes it is necessary *not* to tell your math teacher that you're grumpy, tired, and desperately in need of a tampon because you just got your period. The correct answer to her simple "How are you today?" may just happen to be, "Oh, I'm fine thanks. And you?" But the key is acknowledging the masks we wear and realizing when we have them on, instead of assuming that they reflect our true selves.

Where and with whom are you able to be your most genuine self? One day in seventh grade, I figured it out. After one particularly bad day at school (I think two of my former best friends were leaving me out again), I came to the realization that it was only at home and at my summer theater camp that I felt comfortable being my most genuine self. In those two places, I was imperfect and funny, loud and quiet, I was strut-into-a-room confident and despairingly shy when it came to crushes. I was emotionally honest, deeply trusting, and unendingly loyal. In those places, I didn't have to worry about being cool; instead, I could be authentic.

So here is my two-step advice:

1. Pause (right now, on the couch, in your bed, or wherever you are) and try to identify your most authentic self. For me, it's often a self and a way of being that I can *feel* in my body (there's that doll in your pocket again), a trusting relaxation. Remember the places and people with whom you are able to be that self. When and where does she show her face?

2. Once you've located her and remembered what it *feels* like to be that authentic person, or heard the belly laugh of your most relaxed, REAL self, you can set off in hot pursuit! We can and *must* consciously invest more time and energy in those places, friendships, communities, and activities that allow us to be our unmasked, truest selves. We must *listen* to the happiness we feel when we are allowed to be just *us*.

It's hard, brave, and scary *work* to track down a safe place and authentic expression of your true self. It is also important work—dare I even say essential work? I've found that I'm truly happiest when I am . . . just me. Today, I'll take the deep, honest, imperfect realness of my life just as it is over a people-pleasing, inauthentic mask any day. What a relief!

Of course, sometimes I forget this. And so I keep a quote by Anna Quindlen, an award-winning journalist, author, and all-around cool woman, above my desk. The quote reads:

The thing that is really hard, and really amazing, is giving up on being perfect and beginning the work of becoming yourself.

Maybe she can help you remember, too.

DEFINE: Rupture

To break or burst suddenly; a crack, tear, fracture, or split

---

DEFINE: Repair

To fix, mend, or correct; to make good; to restore by replacing a part or putting together what is torn or broken

---

Just as there is no perfect body and no perfect girl, there certainly can be no "perfect relationship." It simply doesn't exist. Instead, psychologists say that the deepest and best relationships (and that doesn't mean just friendships; these can also be with a parent or in a romantic relationship) are not hanging out in alleged argument-free paradise; instead, they are always evolving. In that evolution and over time, there can be complexities, disagreements, and moments of disconnect. But when you evolve, you grow to the next level of trust and understanding through a bumpy process that psychologists call *rupture and repair*. You fight, then you work it out; you have a dumb, frustrating miscommunication, then you clear it up; and so on. The process of rupture and repair builds *trust*. Over time in a relationship, we hope to learn that "no matter what," we will always figure out the conflicts and roadblocks that get in our way. And then, in some awful times, there is a rupture you can't seem to repair, and the relationship as you knew it is over. It is sad when a friendship is changing for the worse or a romantic relationship is ending. I know I always end up crying a bit, mourning things that were so great in the past but that no longer exist. And yet, often out of this new distance comes a secret relief, as well as space for a new evolution and cycle of our lives.

There are many different ways to "repair" a relationship. I bet you can run through the most clichéd of them in your head: crooning love songs beneath open windows, sending a cheesy card, and so on. But the most tried-and-true, in my opinion, is communication—just plain-old talking it out.

Good communication gets rid of misunderstandings and hurtful assumptions, though it may not get rid of fundamental disagreements. And that is okay. I suggest you challenge yourself to talk frequently and honestly with your closest friends and family, instead of letting things simmer until you're ready to explode. Explosions in close relationships will never be pretty, and they often do the kind of damage that was intended in the moment but that makes the repair afterward really, really hard or maybe even impossible. If you think exploding at your friend would be incredibly satisfying, ask yourself if your momentary satisfaction is worth the friendship.

The idea of *repair* in a friendship is decidedly *not* a little-kid kind of thing. The concept of working, maybe even preventively, to be a better friend is entirely new to the teenage years, and it's an essential tool for surviving the adult ones (though some people never quite seem to manage it, gosh darn it). Repairing after a rupture means being our most *emotionally intelligent* selves. Often it requires that we reach across a divide. This can be exceptionally hard for me to do, especially because I am—and I know this to be true—*always right* (joking!). For me, it is often like pulling teeth to admit that I messed up in a friendship. But the terrible truth is out: I am not perfect. Shucks.

It can be hard not to dive into black-and-white thinking, painting oneself as either the ultimate loser villain or the completely blameless saint. Sometimes after we screw up, it's a real temptation to start declaring that we're *the worst* friend in the world, that it's *all* our fault, and that we just hope against hope that one day our friend will forgive us. Maybe this total humiliation and metaphorical (or even literal) prostration on the ground at their feet will make the pain (that twisting in our gut) go away. But in the world of reality, there are almost infinite shades of gray to every situation, and it was probably a little bit of everyone's fault. We are neither perfect nor despicably evil; we are something called *human*. Welcome to the real world of evolving people.

All of these big friendship concepts aside, sometimes our situation is so specific or so gut-wrenching that what we really need is some *good advice* from a mentor.

DEFINE: Mentor

A trusted friend, counselor, or guide; an adviser, often older, with more experience than the person she's advising

Examples: Obi-Wan Kenobi mentored Anakin Skywalker; Albus Dumbledore mentored Harry Potter; Merlin mentored King Arthur; Glinda mentored Dorothy

Since I cannot personally jump out of this page and talk out the details of your story with you (though I wish I could), I suggest you find someone who can. Find someone *older* than you (because the wisdom of experience, even if it's only a few years' experience, really does make a difference). Find someone who you respect, who you can be open with, who doesn't have an agenda in the situation, who is just there to listen to you, and then . . . *TALK*. Talk about your daily ups and downs and the things that frighten you the very most (death, the dark, being alone). Find a time and place to figure out your most frustrating, confusing, painful situations, and, yes, vent about the friends who are really pissing you the heck off—especially if you are confronted with a situation where someone is being straight-up mean.

Maybe this mentor person is your mom—often moms can be the most unconditionally loving and agenda-less people to talk to (as long as you have an agreement that what you confess to her won't make it back to your friends' moms—a situation that, yet again, requires *trust*). However, if that idea makes you a little bit queasy and you can't begin to imagine talking to your mom in this way, then *find another adult you can talk to.* Maybe it's an older sister or an aunt, or a godmother or a teacher, or a friend's mom or a school guidance counselor, or a therapist or a grandmother, a rabbi or a minister, or a camp counselor or a sports coach or a choir director. You get the idea. Older friends can give you the kind of advice you need—the kind that we all need! But not all "adults" have this wisdom, so find one who does. I know you know the difference.

As much as I love my friends, I do not trust their judgment *all* of the time. Just as I don't always know what's right, neither do my friends, but that doesn't mean they're any less *awesome*. It's just that I sometimes feel that I need an adult's opinion on my situation: maybe a friend's depression has gotten really serious, or the bullying has crossed a line and needs to be dealt with *now*. We shouldn't (nor do we have to) tackle the ups and downs of the teenage years alone. Find someone you respect and get her (or him) in your corner. You can do it on your own terms. Decide what you need in order to feel comfortable talking to this person. Is it absolute confidentiality? Is it a willingness to listen to your whole story or dilemma without interruption? Or perhaps you have an agreement for them not to give advice until you specifically request it? Figure out what you need, and then ask for it. And if you are actually lucky enough to have this conversation with your mom, then (bonus points!) you are officially *daughtering*!

DEFINE: Role Model

A person looked up to by others as an example to be imitated.
This individual does not need to be living in order to be a role model.
It may be a mentor or a person at a distance.

For example, Rosa Parks inspires many to find the strength
to stand up for their own beliefs and human dignity. Gandhi inspires
nonviolence in the face of conflict. Hillary Clinton is a role model
to many women in political leadership. My godmother is a role
model of calm and kindness in the face of overwhelm,
my older cousin is my role model for confidence in her body, and so on.

While we're on the subject of mentoring and older friends, it's important to remember that there are all different forms of friendship. Yes, there's the kind we've already talked about— the straightforward ones with girls our own age who are going through the same stuff that we're going through at the same boy-obsessed, grade-focused, body-changing time. No getting around it, there is something insanely powerful and instantly connect-ing about tackling life's teen hurdles at the same time. There's just less explaining to do. You naturally move at a similar rhythm and speed, have a similar ease with technology, and can be comrades in the trenches of love (or crush) relationships. Your teen buddies get your emotional ups and downs like no one else because, well, they're living it, too.

Yet there are also friendships to be found tucked inside of other kinds of relationships: a friendship found with a grandparent, or a teacher, or a little sister, for instance. I think we often brush aside these other less-conventional friends, who may have the wonderful ability to truly "get" us, in favor of more expected friendships. But what a loss!

Some of my best friends are in this "different" or "special" category. Like my former camp counselor, who is *only* ten years older than I am, and who wears superhero shirts, calls me his little sister, and threatens to beat up any boys who "mess with me." Another friend is sixty years older than I am; she's my French supergranny, Perrine, whom I adopted when I was fifteen. She teaches me how to cook things like shrimp, quizzes me on my latest ups and downs in love, and calls herself my fairy godmother. Yet another is my eight-year-old neighbor, Lucia, who so meticulously instructs me on how to knit a hat, asks me openly about death, and shows me the very meaning of strength as she travels alone across the world each summer to live with her dad in a different country and a different culture. Some of my tightest, mightiest friends are, believe it or not, boys. I have a special band of brothers who hug me, tease me, and give me the best no-nonsense advice a girl could ask for. Some of my dearest friends are gay, and some are questioning the idea of gender altogether. One of my friends is a former teacher. One is a friend's mom. To me, friendship has become fundamentally about trust and authenticity (which you probably already figured out about me). The more viewpoints I can get on this messy, beautiful life, the better.

Rachel, a perky redhead I met when I was teaching a workshop this past summer in California, nervously explained to the circle of girls that all of her best friends were adults. "I sing in my local church's choir, and I've met some really amazing people there." Was she *weird*? she asked. Absolutely not, in my humble opinion. Average? Nope, not that either. She's just doing what feels right to *her*, what works for *her*. Let's face it, folks, when we're looking for true-blue friends, the real thing, we must honestly consider the idea that teens aren't the only place to look. Help *yourself* out and draw the circle of friendship around you as wide as possible.

DEFINE: Bravery

Courageous behavior or character

We as a generation—the Millenials—are the first to mix friendship and the Internet. Yes, ladies, we've got to mention it! For what would our friendships be without the magic intimacy of Facebook posts, texts, and video chats (or whatever newfangled thing has taken over the next crew of younglings by the time you read this book!)? It connects us across geographic gaps and provides a never-ending stream of communication, even after we've left school for the day or for the whole summer. I see it as both a thrilling tool to be harnessed and a dangerous pit of inauthenticity to avoid, for all too often the world of the Internet is an area where the fake takes dominion over the REAL.

I have found that the wide world of Internet friendships gives us a certain kind of freedom, so that we are often bolder than we would be in a face-to-face conversation—sharing photos, secrets, crushes, or sexy conversation. Have you noticed? I have found that people often bend the truth or even tell straight-out lies just for the rush of being that *daring*. But then, the next morning, when they wake up and have to walk into school, the cold light of day (and reality) begins to sink in . . . Ooops!

Although we may feel that we know someone based on how clever or daring they are in front of a keyboard, I believe that in reality, we can never really *know* a person without making actual eye contact, without reading her (or his) body language (how and when they cross their arms or shift their weight from foot to foot, and so on). There are *so* many more layers to communication than we can tell through a message or even on a screen, no matter how good the video-chat connection is.

It's time to get real and admit that Internet friendships require that we walk a fine line between fantasy and reality. I believe we have to find a way to recognize this miracle of a super-fun, faraway-friendship-enabling tool for just what it is: a tool. I think it's quite good for a long-distance chat, staying connected to someone you miss terribly, or sharing photos of someone's fabulous birthday party (how *cute* is that dress??). But it's *not* a useful tool for building and maintaining deep, heart-to-heart friendships. For that, I believe you need the trust and authenticity that the Internet just cannot provide. I have a number of friends who I know will disagree with me, as they have made many a close friend on Internet chat rooms or secure fan sites. But I would argue that it was when they met these friends in person at last—or even looked them in the face over Skype—that a real bond began to take place. You need to be in real time, face-to-face, and be able to reach out and give your real friend a real human hug.

And I'm not the only one who thinks so. Here's a piece of wisdom from a source that many of you—maybe all of you—will recognize:

> Piglet sidled up to Pooh from behind. "Pooh?" he whispered.
> "Yes, Piglet?"
> "Nothing," said Piglet, taking Pooh's hand. "I just wanted to be sure of you."

Let's be sure.

6

Daughtering

....

*Parents can only give good advice or put [their
children] on the right paths, but the final forming
of a person's character lies in their own hands.*

—ANNE FRANK

DEAR GIRL READER—OR MORE TO the point, dear *daughter* reader—at
long last the fateful moment has arrived. You can no longer avoid
the delicious topic that likely made you roll your eyes as your
mom handed you this book: "Honey! A book that will help us be
closer!" It's time to talk about moms! Oh, gosh. Perhaps by now
you thought you had gotten off easy. Wrong.

We've spent the past five chapters of this book, plus an entire
introduction, talking about various important topics for getting
our girl game together: dark nights of the soul; intuition (and the
doll in your pocket); trust; red tent pitching; first periods; falling
in love; the fantastic relativity of ideal beauty; the real definitions
of "fat"; how insanely important it is to *just keep talking* (and face-
to-face please—none of the false bravery of texting); *rupture and
repair;* physical inheritance (yes, *that* butt); emotional inheritance

(the way and the why of how you cry); emotional intelligence; and what being REAL and authentic does for our happiness, trust, and maybe even for our soul. Whew! We've covered some ground. If you want more, check out my daughtering resources online at motheringanddaughtering.com/daughteringresources.

So now it's time to pause, take a breath, and pat ourselves on the back for all of the learning and deep thinking we've done together. And *then* let's make an about-face and apply all of this—everything we've discussed and pondered and learned about ourselves and our friendships—to our relationship with our mom. Yes, I mean that woman who has the impressive and utterly unique ability to both embarrass you and love you more than any other individual in the world, and the one you would love to love back forever (face it), if only she could *get* you, was slightly cooler, would stop using the word "hook up" to mean "meet up," would hover less, and was able to read your mind more (explaining can be *so* aggravating, you know?). If only she was, you know, perfect. That's all.

Because of her imperfections (no worse than anyone else's, for sure), my mom has lived through a level of emotional acting out through my teen years that I would never, ever dare inflict on another human being. Maybe you can relate. With my dear mom, I can be (and often was) my very worst of selves. She has collected more eye rolls, more looks of disgust, more furiously closed doors, and more long periods of grumpiness than any other friend, acquaintance, or family member—and for no other reason than my knowing that I can behave that way and she'll still love me. Did she deserve this treatment? Oh gosh, no.

My relationship with my mom over the past eight years—let's say the teen years—has been one big *paradox* (yes, that chapter 1 word again!) of mortification and love, of embarrassment and deepest gratitude, of frustration and trust. Of course, I love her—she's my mom! I am deeply thankful for so many of the little things she did and does for me: the lunches packed for school, the zillions of trips to dance rehearsals, and feeding my friends. And yet, I have also spent a chunk of the past eight years of my life doing these standard daughter routines: huffing sarcastically when she picks up chicken drumsticks with her hands (how *rude!*), rolling my eyes to the upper reaches of my cranium as she asks my friends who they're dating; employing my favorite surly "whatever" and "fine" with a committed regularity; and letting the *MOMMMM* shriek escape my lips whenever she does anything that could even *possibly* be seen as uncool or stupid. In fact, I have spent whole sadistic afternoons answering her in monosyllables when I knew that all she wanted to do was connect with me. I have learned to make her feel like a complete idiot with one piercing look, and on certain moody mornings, I have done my very best to provoke her as only a daughter can, just to prove my powers. I'm sure that living with me has been at times like walking on eggshells: one false move (one wrong question, one too many reminders to do my homework, one lame usage like "the IM") and darn girlie, you've got yolk all over your feet.

I came to discover that the very thing I prided myself on most in my friendships—my empathy, my ability to listen without judgment, my good humor, my loyalty and protectiveness—often disappeared when I was interacting with my mom. I could so easily become the Other Eliza—the moody, petty, selfish Eliza. But just because I *could* be that way and *was* that way sometimes, did it mean I *had* to be that way? Did I have any choice about who I could be? Couldn't I be better than that, at least now and then?

I wanted to change things not just for her, but for myself, too. It's not *that* fun to fight.

DEFINE: Mortification

Great embarrassment and shame

Have you ever paused and wondered why your mom manages to embarrass you more than any other living creature on this earth? Why she seems to have this mysterious power? I wanted to understand what made me so very irrationally mortified with the way she blows her nose and talks to complete strangers in the grocery line. (She's not *me*, so why do I care so much?) When my friend Linda's wacky mom sings along to the car radio, I think it's funny, and I usually join right in (as Linda pleads "No!"). But when it's my mom? I'm reduced to a blushing red lump, twitching with embarrassment in the front seat. Why? Well, because she's *my* mom, and in many ways, she's an extension of me. Or I am of her. Whatever. You get the picture. It can be very confusing, this mother-daughter thing.

What helped me get over my embarrassment of her was the simple truth of our different identities. I had a realization: my mom and I are actually two different people. That sounds really obvious, I know, but it's the other half of that thought that was like a big lightbulb going off in my head: she's her own person, AND SO AM I. I AM NOT MY MOTHER. The way she chooses to behave is the way *she* chooses to behave. I don't behave that way. The way she behaves doesn't actually reflect on me. I can't tell you how freeing that was once I actually understood and experienced it.

DEFINE: Mood Swings

Abrupt and apparently unaccountable change of emotional states

Have you ever noticed that *click* inside of you that happens when your mood turns, in the space of a millisecond, from giddy to grumpy? I can always feel it—something just *pissed me the heck off*. I never paid that much attention to what had prompted the mood change. I just knew smoke was coming out of my ears, and you'd better back away or get your head bitten off. (Not really.

I'm being dramatic.) The best my mom could hope for from me was a steaming silence. And yet it freaked me out that my entire mood could change so completely without my planning it or even knowing why. I felt out of my own control, trapped in a gloomy mood with no escape route. Once I took the time to think about this, I knew I didn't like it. Trust me, it was so much more *fun* to be in a good mood.

And so I started to ask a very basic question: *Why?* What *specific* thing had changed my mood and made the darkness descend? Was it something my mom had said? Or maybe our future plans had shifted, and I didn't like it? Or was it an association with something unpleasant that had happened earlier in the week? Once I'd hit upon my trigger, I then had to go to that deeply honest place and ask myself whether the mood change was really worth it. Was whatever caused the shift worth being in a funk about or taking it out on the people I happened to be with? Often just understanding *why* my mood had shifted was enough for me to muscle myself out of it. "Come on, Eliza, that's pathetic. You were having so much fun before."

As I grow up, I want to *get it,* I want to be conscious, I want to try to be a better self. What if, as I do with my best friends, I could seek to *repair* after an inevitable *rupture,* without waiting for my mom to come find me? What if I tried to understand the kind of mom my grandma was and how that shaped my mom when she was my age? In a culture where mom-bashing seems to slip off the tongue and flow through the halls of middle school, it can seem bizarre to try to talk or even think with compassion about our mothers. Sometimes it feels like we're *supposed* to not get along with them. But I don't want to give up on my soft, smart, squishy, lovable, goofy, feelingful, hardworking, yummy-food-cooking mom. *I want to change our relationship to fit me.* I don't want to shut down the moment I get home. I want to find a balance between independence and connection, togetherness and solo-time—one that works for *me.*

I am learning that however psychic my mom is (and sometimes she seems to know more than I realize), she can't read my mind. I *do* have to explain things to her with actual words like a normal person—like how I'm feeling, or why I'm feeling that way, or why such and such a word isn't appropriate to use anymore, or which political candidate I support and why. And if I get home from school in the afternoon and all I want is to be alone, in my bed, with a good book, then maybe, just maybe, I will have the maturity to tell her I need a little space. And you know what, ladies? To me, *this* is what daughtering looks like. It's the creation of a relationship that works for me and for us. (Did I mention that this is also way more fun?)

DEFINE: Daughtering

Being active in your relationship with your mom so that she knows the real you; balancing your independence with a dependable bond as you grow into your true self

Just as there are stereotypes of teenage girls (mean, mean, *mean*) and stereotypes of vegetarians (crunchy, fruity hippies), old cat-loving ladies (totally off their rockers), and Wall Street CEOs (modernized evil incarnate), there are also stereotypes of teenage *daughters*. At the most basic level, stereotypes make things easier for our brains: by quickly sorting the constant incoming flood of information (check the box for self-absorbed teen girl), we can dismiss this person or subject and move on. A lot of the time, we don't even realize we're fitting the new kid at school or the stranger on the bus into a neat little box until we've already locked them into the appropriate category in our mind.

But I want to reframe the whole idea of teenage daughters, and I need your help here. I want to change not only the language *about* teenage girls but also the actions available to us. As an example, take the cultural message: "Teenage daughters are impossible and they exhaust their mothers." Let's try this simple reframing: We're not totally exhausting; we're energetic, feisty, and passionate about a lot of things—isn't that something to celebrate? And if someone says that we're "always distracted," maybe it's just because we feel kind of overwhelmed by the information that is available to us, the state of our world, and the heaps of expectations layered on us. But you know what? We take breaks from that, too, and we can focus with intensity on anything we really *love*.

So then, are teen daughters "impossible"? No, we are a fresh challenge. Try this:

> Hey, Mom [yes, *her*, your mom, on the other side of this book], I want a new kind of relationship and some kind of *real* change that acknowledges that I'm not a little kid anymore. And I'm not talking about you getting teary as you remember me in diapers and now here we are buying bras together. I'm talking about a change *in the way you think about me*. If I'm willing to see you as *your* own separate person, can you be willing to see me as *my* own separate person? One who might just be capable of flashes of more maturity than you give me credit for, even if I'm not demonstrating it 100 percent of the time?

I've been gathering teenage daughters' definitions of the new term *daughtering* over the past few years. I want us to revolutionize ourselves out of passivity—the unfortunate recipients of our annoying mothers' attentions—and into action. Here are some of my favorite definitions from the daughters I know:

Daughtering is the act of showing your mom the world with fresh eyes.

Daughtering is realizing your mom is a person just like you.

Daughtering is honest love.

Daughtering is the job of blossoming, growing, like a flower.

Daughtering is the act of loving your mom and then having a
daughter and loving her and then her having a daughter and
loving her, and so on . . .

Daughtering is making orderly lists to organize the clutter around
my house that frustrated me so much as a kid.

It seems to me that when given the chance, teen girls define
daughtering along the lines of *vision, identity,* and *action.* We
have unique insights into the world *and* into our own family,
specifically the line from mother to daughter to mother to
daughter—or the matriline. We are working hard to figure out
who exactly we want to be and sort through how it corresponds
and doesn't correspond to our mom. And above all it is something that we consciously *do,* each and every day: we *daughter.*
We have the potential here, in the midst of the teen years, to take
this matriline into our own hands: the patterns we choose, the
conversations we dive into, and the life we make. We may even
be so bold as to change the course of the lives of women who
have come before us. (Have you changed your grandma's mind
about something recently?)

Because daughtering is fundamentally about *action,* it might
be useful to have some action guidelines. These are some of the
tools I have used and continue to use to this day.

Guidelines for Daughtering

1. **Don't give up on your mom.** Giving up is when you say, "She'll
   never get me, she'll *never* trust me, she'll *always* embarrass me."

2. **Stay real.** Be authentic and genuine. Cut the BS.

3. **Build the relationship YOU want and need**—the one where she actually listens when you're talking and you actually want to listen back. A relationship that looks like, you know, two people getting along.

4. **Accept the fact that your mom is just another person.** She's human, however much she may try to hide it. This means that (1) she will make mistakes, and (2) she can (and should) be on that wonderful, terribly challenging personal journey to be her best possible self and best possible mother.

5. **Realize what you are internalizing and choose which pieces you want.** Look up your matriline and try to fully understand the lives that your mom, grandmas, and great-grandmas have lived. Ask questions and discover the real *her*stories. If you know what is being handed down, you can start to choose what you want to carry on with you and what you want to remember to leave behind.

6. **If necessary, find a mom, any mom, who can give you the mothering you need.** This steady, dependable bond with an adult, and often an adult woman, is something that we daughters *need* during the teen years. If your mom—bless the cause and effect that has made her who she is—is unable to give you this, find someone who can. No, this is not the next episode of "Mom Swap," nor are you "giving up your mom" (sorry, she's always going to be your mom). You are seeking the support that YOU need. It's called "community." They're called "village mothers." Have you heard the expression, "It takes a village to raise a child"? Well, I think that's true. If your mom can't give you the mothering you need, then find another mother in your "village" (the community that extends outside your family) to fill

in the blanks. You deserve it. You can *daughter* people other than your mother.

We teen daughters have a unique perspective as we look up the matriline. I believe that part of our daughtering reaches up past our own mom to our grandma and her mom before her. What has been passed down, and what needs to be forgiven? I will never forget the conversation I had with my Mimi, my mom's mom, the Christmas when I was sixteen. That was when she told me about her mom, who, just like mine, was also named Priscilla. Priscilla was a lifelong invalid, always in and out of bed and on the way to doctors' appointments to deal with her asthma (back then, there wasn't a treatment for it, except to move to a warmer climate and hope for the best). To keep his job, her husband, my great-grandpa Ned, had to live far away. My own Mimi loved to ride horses as a girl, and from the age of six, she took lessons almost every afternoon. But her mom was allergic to horses, and so every evening, as my grandmother went for her daily visit to Priscilla's bedside, she had to first be scrubbed from head to toe. And that made me wonder, sitting on the couch that Christmas Eve, what does that do to a little girl? What would that do to a child, not to be able to just run in to her mother and give her a hug or have her mom seek her out for some spontaneous fun? What would it do to a child not to be able to bake cookies with her mom or sit on her lap for a story or be tucked in by her at night? What did it do to my Mimi? And how did that affect the way she mothered *my* mom? And how did that affect the way my mom mothered me?

Priscilla died at forty-seven years old, when my Mimi was only twenty-five and recently married. On the day that Mimi told me the story, I was able to see a small piece of what her own inheritance was, what my mom's had become, and therefore what mine is today. And that realization and acceptance, that understanding that you and your mom are part of a much larger whole, that is also what daughtering is about.

DEFINE: Rejection

The dismissing or refusing of an idea or person,
or the spurning of a person's affections

The last big question about teenage daughters that I am left with is this (and this is not the first time you've heard it): Do we need to reject our mothers in order to grow up and become our fully independent selves? If we *don't* push them away—and I mean as far away as emotionally possible—will our identity and path to true adulthood be stunted and undermined *forever?* Will we be the lost little children who never quite grew up? Will we identify too much with our mom and never become a fully developed, unique person? Let's unpack this one carefully.

Psychologists have been declaring for years that the famous "tension" (ahem, *fighting*) of the teen years is natural, normal, and necessary. "Don't take it personally!" our mothers are told. "ALL teenagers scream 'I hate you' and slam the door. It's a rite of passage! Don't hold them back by insisting that they stay in relationship with you, you selfish mother, you."

Well, after years of being a teenage daughter and working with teenage daughters, my conclusion is this: rejection is different from resistance. There is a natural resistance that occurs in the mother-daughter relationship as the daughter begins to make the transition from child to adult. This tension can be found in everything from curfews to clothes, from political opinions to beliefs about sex. But fundamentally it's about: *Who am I? Who are you? And how can I make sure we're not the same?* It's that natural tension between an independent and an enmeshed identity. There's a push and a pull and a crucial redefining and restructuring of the relationship that needs to happen during the teen years, because, guess what? One of you isn't the same anymore and that changes both of you forever.

So the rejection myth is just that, a myth. In fact, I believe that having a connected relationship with your mom is one of the best predictors of being a sane and stable adult.

DEFINE: Identity Crisis

A period of uncertainty and confusion in which a person's sense of identity becomes insecure, typically due to a change in their expected aims or role in society

I want to tell you a story, just as I did in chapter 1. But this time, instead of Vasilisa the Wise, I want to talk about Persephone, the Queen of the Otherworld. (If you've studied any Greek mythology, you may know her as the Queen of the *Under*world.) Just like Vasilisa, Persephone is a girl who lived perhaps two thousand years ago, or maybe she didn't live at all. Her story, passed on from generation to generation, can be a metaphor for our own lives and can offer a different way of understanding the ups and downs, twists and turns of the path before us—from home to school, from school to basketball practice, from practice to next Friday's party. One of the reasons we love stories (as children and, *yes*, even up into our preteen and teen years) is because we can pretend to be our favorite characters, we can try on the arc of their lives—or, simply put, we can relate.

I first heard the story of Persephone in fifth grade when my middle-school class did a unit on Greek myths. As with many old stories, specifically the ones that have made it into the history books of the Western world, the tale of Persephone has been written and rewritten, translated and interpreted from its original Greek by . . . men. Mostly older white men.

Now I'm not going to condemn the whole lot of them (in fact, I have a fairly wonderful specimen of their kind for a dad), but

I'm of the opinion that looking at the story of Persephone from this one viewpoint is narrow-minded and definitely *not* true to my take on the world. In fact, it's interesting to remember that these same minds happen to have written down most of our recorded history and stories. (Hmmm, how does that fact shape our world history and our modern reality?) So those of you who have heard the story before may notice that I have taken some creative license with it. You see, I want to make it *our* story. So, yes, you know what to do now: get cozy, snuggle up, and let's talk about Persephone, the ultimate teenage girl and the ultimate teenage daughter.

Persephone
Queen of the Otherworld

Once there was a little girl named Kore (pronounced "Corrie") who lived with her mother, Demeter, the goddess of grain and growth, in a small cottage overlooking a grassy meadow. Every day as Demeter began her daily tasks, young Kore ran out to play with her friends, the flower nymphs, in the neighboring hills, fields, rivers, and valleys that were their playground. The days became weeks and the weeks long years, and Kore grew into a beautiful young woman. Yet still each morning, she rose early, faithfully bid her hardworking mother good-bye, and went to play, sing, and gather flowers with her companions, the nymphs.

One such morning, as they gathered in the valley of a gurgling river, Kore wandered farther and farther from her friends, down along the grassy riverbanks. And there among the bulrushes, she noticed a white bud, just breaking into flower as its stem rose from the mud at the edge of the river. Kore knelt in the wet earth to pluck it, and suddenly the bank side burst open, and out of the darkness burst a golden chariot pulled by two fierce black stallions. At the helm was a towering young man in billowing dark robes. In that single moment, Kore realized one thing: gosh, he was CUTE. His strong arms grasped her and pulled her back into the gaping blackness. The passage closed behind them, and outside, the river calmly continued to wend its way along, obscuring the path of Kore's muddy footprints.

Demeter was desolate. All work halted, and she spent her days wandering the barren earth, calling Kore's name over and over again to the dark hills and winding valleys. The weeks passed, and still she mourned her child.

Down in the darkness, in a world so different from the sunny, grassy one of Kore's childhood, Kore sat enthroned in a palace of stone. At her side was Hades, the young man in black robes whose strong arms had first pulled her from her mother's world. He swore his love for her and led her through the twisting passages and dark caverns that made up his underground world. He wished to make her his queen. And Kore, in love with this new place, accepted, and became Persephone, no longer a young girl but Queen of the Otherworld and a goddess in her own right. But every now and then, she thought of her mother, above the soil on sunny Earth, and she missed their laughter, their childhood snuggles, the warm foods, and the peaceful fields.

So one day Persephone told Hades that she would like to go above the darkness of their world to visit her mother. He agreed, but first gathered her close to him and offered her the ruby seeds of a pomegranate that grew in his gardens. Persephone ate six seeds, which quickly stained her lips a deep red. Marked like this, as a being of the Otherworld, she rose above the soil to see her mother again.

Demeter rejoiced to have her daughter in her arms again. For two long weeks they roamed the sunny hillsides, hand in hand, no longer a mother with her child, but two women, one young, one old. This time when Persephone bid her mother good-bye and descended again to the Otherworld, she promised to return. And so six months of each year, Persephone dwells in the darkness under the earth as Queen, and Demeter's world grows cold and barren, and for all humans, it becomes winter. Then in the spring, Persephone climbs to the surface of her mother's meadows, and, with joy, Demeter sends fresh life to the tips of every tree and into the root of every flower, and the world blossoms again. Persephone found the balance of these comings and goings, and so the seasons were born.

Like Persephone, our life as daughters (and as girls and as people on this earth) is about finding the balance of "comings and goings," of being able to exist in the paradox that is the natural love and tension of the mother-daughter relationship during the teen years. We have our childhood world—often the world of our mother (or of Demeter)—and we have our own world, the "Otherworld" of which Persephone is Queen. This Otherworld is so different from our mom's reality that she usually has to work hard to even understand it.

"Otherworld" language and its nuances can be a source of confusion for her. On more than one occasion, I've had to explain to my mom the difference between a text and an online IM or to remind her of the correct definition of "hipster" when she starts using the term to describe certain hats, pop stars, and friends of mine. And you and your mom may have very different meanings assigned to slang words. Like, I let the term "suck" trip off my tongue on the regular: this homework *sucks*, this rainy weather *sucks*, my gym teacher totally *sucks* (he made me do two extra laps today), and so on. But my mom draws a shocked breath ("Eliza!"), because for her, *suck* refers to a very literal sexual act and is not in the realm of casual exchanges or grumpy complaints about life. And "hooking up"? Yeah, that means "meeting up" to my mom. Now let the hilarity ensue . . . Are we hooking up later? *No mom, we are definitely not.* This is what I mean by the confusion of the Otherworld.

But the idea of Otherworld also goes deeper. When you leave your "mother's world," you also leave your childhood world (that closed, lovely reality) and begin to branch out on your own. It may almost seem to your mother as if you've "disappeared," like Kore. ("What's come over you? I hardly know you anymore!") You discover new favorite foods that your mom has never tried and new types of music that your mom doesn't even know how to pronounce. But these little preferences are indicators of something bigger: you are not a child tripping around your mom's ankles anymore; you are very much your own person—and she is trying to adjust and hopefully learn to acknowledge it.

Until the time we hit the teenage years (or maybe the preteen years), our reality, our opinions, and even our emotions are intrinsically linked to those of our mom. Remember when you were scared just because your mom was scared? And how sad and uncomfortable seeing your mom cry made you feel—and still may make you feel now? And how automatically her opinions were your own (from food to politics to answers on the ultimate question about God—don't forget that this was your first reality)? The Otherworld, this new stage in our lives, is about being able to politely (and sometimes not so politely) disagree on everything from politics to religion to how you like your eggs cooked in the morning. It is about being able to be okay when your mom is sad or struggling or hurting (proving that she, too, is a real person). It's about seeing the world with fresh eyes, with the vision of someone waking up in a new land—the land of adulthood rather than of childhood. It's about looking for a balance between your need for independence and your need to have a reliable, strong bond with your mom.

DEFINE: Grow

To progress to maturity, to develop, or to produce by cultivation (hard work)

The fact is, if you are reading this book, you already are not a little kid anymore, and so I'm not going to treat you like one. It's that simple. Even though I am likely a few years older than you (who really cares?), I have spent this book talking to you as I would to a friend or a not-much-younger sister. I hate being talked down to (who doesn't?), so I'm not going to do it to you. And since I am not going to treat you like a little kid, don't act like one. You're bigger than that.

Now I've got a challenge for you.

I'm challenging you to choose to consciously *grow*. And I don't mean the narrow-minded "grow *up*" that lectures you to stop crying, stop complaining, and get a job. Just as the way to be trusted is to *earn* trust, to be trust*worthy*, the way to be treated as the young woman you are becoming is to earn that treatment, to prove you're worthy of it.

To me, daughtering is one huge stepping-stone on the path that lies ahead of you. Daughtering is about taking on the challenge of growing up, of living life with your heart, mind, *and* body, of finding that impossibly possible balance of mom and me, of me and others. Growing up into your best and most whole self is not something that passively happens to you. If you sit in a chair in the corner and paint your nails (or twiddle your thumbs) for the next ten years, you will not de facto, instantly, presto, like the next microwavable treat, become a fully cooked "adult." No, growing up for real, on the inside, is something you have to actively take on for yourself. And, girl, is it a challenge?!

I've had a quote tacked on my wall, right above my desk, for the past three years. It's by Anaïs Nin, a brilliant and controversial writer who is most famous for her published (and quite racy) diaries:

And the time came when the risk it took to remain tight
in a bud was more painful than the risk it took to blossom.

What she says (in beautiful metaphor) is that we are the bud and we could be the blossom. To me, this eloquently sums up the growing pains of the teenage years, the tension between leaving the security of childhood behind and jumping blindly into the abyss toward adulthood. But this quote, to me at least, also refers to all of the smaller moments along the way when we have a choice—the choice, for instance, to sit a dear friend down for a difficult conversation, knowing, even if it's the "right" thing to do, that it will change your friendship forever. That is a moment in which we can blossom, or we can scrunch up tight in our little bud and refuse to budge, refuse to change or adapt to the moving world around us.

Have you ever had a blossoming moment like this? Or felt what it is to be, metaphorically speaking, wrapped up tight in a bud, terrified to open? What this quote says to me is that sometimes—in fact, almost always—the pain of trying to stay closed and safe is worse than the risk, fear, and potential pain of "breaking open."

You know what? Heck, let's blossom. We may shed a lot of teenage tears along the way, but let's do this thing called life. Let's live it fully and to the best of our ability. And being truly, deeply honest (maybe so honest that it hurts a little bit): Wouldn't it be nice if we could do it with our moms by our sides?

7

Meeting in the Middle

....

Out beyond ideas of wrongdoing
And rightdoing there is a field.
I'll meet you there.

—RUMI

WELCOME, DEAR MOTHER AND DEAR DAUGHTER! This chapter is unlike the others that have come before it because it's written for the two of you to read together—cozied up with hot chocolate, or side by side on the couch, or however *you* like to do it. It's intended to be both a meeting place between the two very different worlds of mothering and daughtering and a miniworkshop, complete with a variety of exercises the two of you can do together. You'll also find a series of conversations, or dialogues (or, ahem, disagreements), between the two of us. The dialogues address some of the most common issues that a preteen and teenage girl can have with her mom. And no surprise, they are all based on real conversations that the two of us have had ourselves, more than once, over the years. The words we use to talk through things may not be the words *you* use to talk through things, but do not be deterred. What we're trying to do here is model a *way* in which you can talk to each other to help you keep your bond strong through the teen years and beyond. Consider this chapter a springboard for your relationship—from the page to your living-room couch—right here, right now.

We like to imagine that all four of us—mother, daughter and mother, daughter—are meeting right now in the lovely "field" that the ancient poet Rumi describes in the excerpt at the start of this chapter. Like the red tent that we build at each of our workshops, Rumi's field is a special place we can enter at any time. In this field, all four of us agree to just let go of (for now!) our old complaints and outdated ideas about each other and to find a place where we don't worry about who is "right" and who is "wrong" in a conversation. Instead, we try to just listen and really *understand* each other. Whenever we can do this, we are able to locate our fundamental bond, the thing that links us so strongly, right underneath the surface of daily squabbles and disagreements. If you already do this a lot—great! Our dialogues and exercises will reinforce what you have. If you aren't able to *really* connect very often or very easily, perhaps some of our dialogues can help you find a way to do so. When we moms and daughters can remember what it feels like to *trust* and to be truly *heard* (on both sides), it is so much easier to work out any problem we are having with each other on any given day.

So, find a quiet spot and at least one hour that you can both commit to, and then shut the rest of the world out. This means locking the door to all siblings; getting away from the computer, video games, and work email; and turning off all phones and other digital devices. Yes, turn them off! You can do it!

Here are a few guidelines for the chapter:

1. Read it *together*, in whichever way works for you: silently and at the same time, or taking turns out loud, or the daughter reading Eliza's parts of the conversation and the mother reading Sil's, or switching it up to have the daughter read

Sil's parts aloud and the mother read Eliza's. Do whatever appeals to you. And naturally you can change your mind anytime you want.

2. If you read something that you find especially interesting, funny, or relevant—or even something that you disagree with—*pause and talk about it*. Always. (This miniworkshop will take more than an hour. But remember, you don't need to read the whole chapter in one sitting.)

3. Have a diary or notepad at your side—one for each of you— as you read.

4. Be *real*—or "authentic" (a mother word)—as you work together through this chapter. The more honesty, respect, and good humor you give to this time together, the more your bond will give you in return. Dear mother, dear daughter: this is the challenge—we know you're ready to bring your best and truest selves to this very last chapter of the book.

DIALOGUE 1: It's Time for Things to Change

Eliza: Ma, *why* do you still treat me like I'm a little kid sometimes? Frankly it's a little insulting—I'm not five.

Sil: I'm sorry that you feel that way. Here's the truth of it: I feel like I'm always trying to catch up with you. I feel that as soon as I get the hang of mothering one version of you, you grow up again. Sometimes I have to catch myself and say, "Oh right, she doesn't need me to make her lunch for school or make sure she's wearing a coat if it's cold." You're feeling that I'm lagging behind a lot lately, aren't you?

Eliza: Heck yes, it's so frustrating. That's why I brought it up! Hello! I feel like you really don't see that I am *different* than I was when I was a little kid.

Sil: Like I said, I keep trying to catch up to your growing-up self. I feel a little sad that I have to let go of this kid who no longer exists, but it's also awesome to me that you're growing up so fast and that you have so many capabilities. It amazes me that you are so fantastically organized and on time, when you know my style is chaotic in comparison.

Eliza: Gosh, Ma. I *had* to be organized. I'm sure I learned it in *reaction* to you. I *know* I'm changing. That's why I want to have this conversation! I think what happens is that I kind of expect you to read my mind, and to, like, psychically, instantly know what I need at any given moment. And if you don't, then instead of talking to you about it, I just get pissed off and am a grump for the rest of the day.

Sil: Yeah. That can get pretty tiring for both of us.

Eliza: I mean, it would be a lot easier if you were superhuman and could read my mind!

Sil: Ah well. The secret's out: I'm not perfect! Okay, so it seems like the bottom line is that it's time for some things to change in our relationship, things that we can and should be consciously aware of—big things and real things.

Eliza: *Yes.* I mean, it's kind of funny, or maybe ironic, but sometimes I act younger than I really am around you—I just act out because I know I can. It's like just being around you can bring out the most childish version of myself. I reserve some of my worst, most selfish, little-kid-tantrum-throwing behavior for you.

Sil: I've noticed. Sometimes, when I'm rested and in balance myself, I give you the space to act out. When I'm tired though—watch out! I think your mom *should* be a person you can go to and be your most honest, grumpy self. But when you're plain *mean* to me—or cross *all* of the time—that's when and where I set my limits. If you want things to be different, then maybe we both need to change a bit?

Eliza: I'm not a little kid, Mom, and I don't want to be treated like one. And I don't really want to act like one, either. So, yeah, maybe we could both work on changing things.

Sil: Good. We'll both try to remember. And when I forget sometimes and treat you like you're younger than you are, you can remind me about our conversation today, and that in itself will show me how quickly you're growing up. How does that sound?

Eliza: Yeah. Just please try to remember. I don't want to have to be the one to keep reminding you. That's kind of obnoxious.

Sil: I will, honey. I promise.

Eliza: Okay, like, for example, when I tell you something that is private, like a secret, please keep it to yourself. It makes me *soooo* mad when you don't do that. You're always talking about "trust, trust, trust," but what if I can't trust you with my private stuff? I am *not* going to tell you what's on my mind if I have to worry that one of my friends' moms is going to find out. Sometimes there are even things that I don't want anyone else in our family to know, not even Dad. If you feel like you want to tell someone something, just ask me! It's simple!

Sil: You are absolutely right to be mad. You need to be able to trust me. It's a good example because it's one of those things about you growing up—when you were little, you didn't have private things that I had to keep to myself. Like last week, I realize that I should never have spoken with Carissa's mom about your very private feeling that you were being left out by the girls at school. I just wasn't thinking. I'm so, so sorry; that information is *yours* to share with who you want. It's not mine. I won't do it again.

Eliza: So can we agree that you'll always ask me first?

Sil: Absolutely. But you know the exception: if you tell me something involving a friend who might do harm to themselves or someone else, then I have to do something about it. This doesn't mean that you shouldn't tell me; in fact, please do tell me. There are certain tough situations you shouldn't have to deal with by yourself. And I promise to always explain to you what I'm doing and why, and we can work out together ahead of time how I am going to handle the problem. I think it comes down to something we've talked about before: privacy versus secrecy. I can absolutely respect your need to have certain things be private, but secrets are never good, for anyone.

Eliza: Okay. But the safety thing is a rare exception. What I'm talking about is treating me like an adult if you truly want me to be one. It's basic respect.

Sil: Absolutely. I appreciate you telling me. I think we can prevent problems here if I always check with you before I talk to someone about what you have shared with me.

Eliza: Deal.

Sil: And I will try to see you for who you are today, and not who you were a year ago.

Eliza: Thanks, Mom. I think that will make a big difference.

Exercise: Share One Idea

Pause and share with each other one of your favorite ideas from Mothering or Daughtering (whichever you have just read). What was an idea, story, or paragraph that particularly stuck with you? Perhaps it was a section that you related to, or maybe it was one that made you think differently. Locate this example and read it out loud. Discuss.

Three-Word Check-Ins: An Exercise in Essence

"How are you?" It's a routine question that we all answer multiple times daily. Often we respond with a monosyllabic "Fine" or "Good" (when frankly the last thing you may be is fine or good). Other times we launch into a long-winded response that covers everything and nothing—like, "Well, I took Charlie to school and then I had to take the dog to the vet, but the appointment was actually at 10:15, and I thought it was at 10:30, so we were late, but luckily . . ." and on and on. May you both—daughter and mother alike—be spared from such shallow babble when all you really want is to connect.

Right now, let's try to do just that—connect. We can do it by answering the everyday "How are you?" differently, perhaps more authentically, in the form of a three-word check-in. This is an exercise in *essence*. How can we get to the essence—the heart of the matter—of how we are feeling in this moment? By checking in with our most honest selves and summarizing how we feel in *just three words*.

Eliza: Right now, I, Eliza, feel "hopeful, frustrated, and reflective." I don't need to explain all of the many reasons exactly *why* I feel those three things, but you *get* it, right? You know what hopeful, frustrated, and reflective *feel* like—and you have an authentic window into my state right now as I sit at my little white desk, typing away on my computer.

Sil: And I feel "anxious, content, and creative." It's important to remember that sometimes our emotions can exist in *paradox:* I can be both content and anxious at the same time. Just speak to the truth of how you feel.

Exercise: A Three-Word Check-In

Take one minute to check in with your most *real* self. How do you feel in this moment? As our daughters have already read about, signals to our emotional truth can often be read in our bodies. So if you're having a hard time pinpointing how you're feeling, check in with yourself physically: How does your chest feel? Your stomach? Your shoulders? Pick three words that communicate your state of being right now— honestly and authentically. Take turns sharing them. No explanation is necessary.

Mothering Guidance: Are You in Crisis?

Are you getting a divorce? Are there substance-abuse problems going on with either of you? Has something happened so that you are barely talking with each other? If you and/or your daughter are in crisis, I recommend you get some extra help right away. Don't delay. A skilled therapist can be a great mediator. Don't be hard on yourself if you need this kind of help! All kinds of resources exist for you, even if you are not insured. Check with your county mental-health program.

DIALOGUE 2: Tackling the Mom Embarrassment Thing

Eliza: Ma, *why* do I get so totally embarrassed by you? Why do you bug me and piss me off more than almost anyone in the whole world? I just get so *frustrated* sometimes! Do you know?

Sil: Yeah, I've noticed! Why do you think it is?

Eliza: I don't know! That's why I'm asking you! I feel kind of guilty about it. Most of the time you don't deserve it, but I can't seem to help myself. Sometimes I judge you so much for the dumbest little things. It's no fun being frustrated by you all the time. I'd rather just get along. What is *up* with this?

Sil: Well, one thing that gets to you big time is that I am not at all shy in the way that, for example, I strike up conversations in public with people I don't know. Because I'm your mom, maybe you're worried people are going to judge you for my behavior?

Eliza: Does it hurt your feelings when I get insanely, turn-bright-red irritated with you, like I do, or when I roll my eyes or treat you like you're, well, stupid?

Sil: Sometimes. Actually, I don't feel hurt as much as I feel sad. I feel sad because when you judge me—and that's what you're doing when you treat me like I'm a complete moron—it's hard not to feel a distance between us. Also, because I have judged *my* mother so much in the past myself—you're not the only one in the universe who's ever done this. Now, here I am the mom, and you're judging me. It's a real adjustment, because just a few years ago there was almost no conflict between us. You know? And I ask myself, just like you do, does it have to be this way?

Eliza: Well, I think it kinda does. I associate myself so much with you that when you do something that I find totally embarrassing, I forget that I'm not the one doing it. Well, no, I don't forget—it just feels like it's just as bad as *if* I were doing it myself.

Sil: You know, Lize, there are times when I want to be cool, but as I get older and I get more comfortable with who I am, I don't feel as much of a need to fit in. Teenagers have so much pressure to conform— your appearance and choices seem to matter on a social level all the time. I think you used to love my outgoing and even goofy side, and now it seems to be the very thing that frustrates you so much.

I used to be a little intimidated by you when you first started copping an attitude with me—right around middle school, I think. Lately, though, I don't feel as though I change who I fundamentally am around you. And I have never tolerated you being mean. Have you noticed that I draw the line there?

Eliza: Yeah. You definitely let me know when I've gone a step too far. I think I snap out of my grumpiness pretty quickly because, as terrible as it sounds, I suddenly remember that you actually have feelings, too. And it's not like you're *trying* to piss me off or anything.

Sil: I think every daughter experiences all of this to some degree— feels that what her mom does reflects on her, that she's an extension of her mom, and one that she can't control particularly well. All this is happening to you just as it happened to me, only we are talking about it in ways Grandma and I never did.

Eliza: It's nice we can talk this way. Not all my friends have this.

Sil: Yeah, I'm glad we can, too. I wouldn't trade this for anything in the world.

Eliza: Mom, I think I need you to just give me some space sometimes. You *do* bug me, and I *do* get grumpy. And then after I've had some time to breathe and thrash around in my bedroom and stare at the ceiling and think and feel guilty, I realize how crazy I can actually be. I guess I have to practice not taking your outgoing, crazy, mortifying behavior as a personal insult or whatever. I'm me and you're you, and I may have a wacky mom, but I can choose to be as "normal" as I like. Or not.

Sil: Exactly. Wacky, normal—you can make your own choices.

Mothering Guidance: To Yell or Not to Yell?

Mothering magazine's Peggy O'Mara answers this question for me with her wise words: "The way we talk to our children becomes their inner voice." (And yes, I have yelled at Eliza, and I have always regretted it. And this has meant that I needed to move on, apologize, forgive myself, keep growing, and put the correction in.)

Tracing Your Matriline

More often than not, the stories of the men in our family trees are valued over those of the women. It's a simple fact. Because they've been allowed to have more public roles in society, their names and their stories are better known. Women have also traditionally taken their husband's family's last name when they marry—another way the matriline can get lost over time. Even if we don't know the exact names of the women who have come before us (and many of us don't), we are honoring their memory when we speak about them and imagine what their lives may have been like.

Eliza used to think that talking about the matriline was, well, a bit nerdy. (Yeah, that's an understatement.) But that was only at first. Now it has become what she calls "a modern act of feminism." We want to know about the women who came before us, who often didn't hold a job and were told they didn't need a formal education.

They may have raised four or six or eight children, though, and we think that's a life's work to be hugely proud of. We *do* want to hear their stories. Don't you?

Exercise: Trace Your Matriline

Part 1: Get out a piece of paper and two pens and draw a tree. This isn't a leafy apple tree with lots of branches; this is a fir tree—a tree that goes straight up. You are tracing your matriline, or the order of ancestors running from mother to mother to mother. Some genealogists call it the *uterine line* (for obvious reasons). Write down the generations as far back as you know, starting with you, dear daughter reader, at the very top. If, as you go further and further down toward the roots, all you know is a nickname, that's fine! If somewhere along the line there are two mothers, or a stepmother, or if you are adopted and know both matrilines, make as many trees and matrilines as you have the information for.

Part 2: Now, Mom, share a story about one of the women on the tree. If possible, tell a story that your daughter hasn't heard before.

Part 3: Mother reader, what was your relationship like with your mom when you were a teen? Was she able to give you what you needed emotionally? Did you talk with her about real things? What did you argue about? How does your relationship with your mom affect your relationship with your daughter, both positively and negatively? Try to find nuggets of truth and avoid generalizations. And daughter reader, do you have any questions you've always wanted to ask your mom about her relationship with her mom?

Part 4: Daughter reader, share about the idea of inheritance discussed in Daughtering, and the conscious choice we have about our generational baggage and our generational gifts. Remember, being conscious and aware is the *challenge* and the choice we all have.

DIALOGUE 3: "I Can't Wait Until I Can Just Do What I Want"

Eliza: Mom, why won't you let me do *anything* I want to do these days? It feels like every time I want to do something new—something that *everyone* else's parents are okay with—you just don't trust me enough. It's really embarrassing, and it pisses me off. I feel like I've done *everything* possible to prove that you can trust me.

Sil: Whoa. Let's back up and start at the beginning. Can we sit down and talk this through?

Eliza: Yeah. But it's not like it's going to make any difference. You don't trust me, and there's nothing I can do about it.

Sil: Well, let's give it a try. We're usually pretty good at talking things through. Now, what is this bit about not letting you do *anything* you want these days?

Eliza: It feels that way.

Sil: Okay. Let's talk through specifics. It seems to me like you've been pretty pissed off ever since Dad and I set the 11:00 p.m. curfew.

Eliza: Yeah. Well, you know ALL my friends have later curfews, and it feels like you guys just don't trust me, and you never will. I don't even know what I did wrong. I am always really careful, and I have never gotten into trouble. Haven't I earned the right to stay out later?

Sil: Yes and no. You have definitely earned our trust, but that doesn't mean we will let you go to just any person's house and come home anytime. For instance, some of your friends are older than you—at least the friends you hang out with on weekends. Daddy and I like your friends—they're good kids. But even good kids can make bad choices sometimes.

Eliza: Mom, it's so frustrating how obsessed you are with my safety! You *know* me; I'm not going to make stupid choices. It's just so obnoxious and embarrassing that I have to leave wherever I am at 11:00! And it's not just that—I feel like you don't trust me about anything else either: you always ask who I'm texting, you always make me give you my Facebook and email passwords. It's like you don't trust me to make good choices.

Sil: Honey, it's not about trust; it's about safety. And we won't always have your passwords. You will grow out of the need for us to oversee this. It's not about *you;* I trust you, and I know you've got a smart head on your shoulders. It's about everyone else out there. In a few more years, you'll stop being a teenager, and you'll move out of this house, and these choices will be all yours. For now, you will have to live with the limits we have set. Please know that we do *know* and trust you. This is not about trust. This is not a personal insult. This is about your health and balance and safety.

Eliza: My health? Oh, please.

Sil: Absolutely. The schedule you keep is crazy; you're exhausted half the time. Between school, homework, dance rehearsals, after-school clubs, work, chores around the house, your friends, your boyfriend, and your family—well, sometimes I have to be the one to set limits or, if possible, to help you set limits. Even when you're back at 11:00 p.m. on a weekend night, you're not asleep until at least midnight, and then you sleep half the day to make up for how tired you are. Or it can be with setting limits around school—when you're overworked and exhausted, you get sick, you get cranky, we don't get along, and your schoolwork suffers.

Honey, growing up is also about finding balance, and I'm trying to show you that, too. Sometimes your schedule is just too much! You are overextending yourself, you are stretched to the max trying to keep up your social life and dance and school. I am sorry, Sweetie, but this is where we draw the line. This is how our family does it. We get to set the limits until you are *really* ready to set them for yourself.

Eliza: Ugh. I can't wait until I can just do what I want!

Sil: I know. But do you get, even just a little bit, how you need to find more balance?

Eliza: I get it. I get it. I just want to be older *now!* Ugh.

Exercise: Your Daughtering Definition

The new word *daughtering* has a deep meaning and implication for both teen daughters and adult daughters (yes, you mothers) alike. First, daughter: What is daughtering to you? After reading all of Eliza's definitions and stories in her chapter 6, how would you define the word? Now, together with your mom, list at least three ways that you already daughter your mom.

Second, mother: What is daughtering to you, as an adult daughter? How has your relationship changed with your mom since you were a teen? What are at least three ways that you daughter your mom? (Does your daughter have any ideas? She's seen you with Grandma.) What is at least one way that you could daughter her more? Even if she has already passed away, there is still daughtering work to be done. For example, what have you *internalized* from your mother? Work with that inner mother instead. You might write to your mother in your journal, for instance, and tell her things you wish you had told her when she was alive. This can be a very healing process.

THE COMMUNICATION TOOLBOX

We're getting ready for some nitty-gritty conversations (oh boy, right?). Here are our favorite rules and tools for effective communication. And guess what? They work. And they can actually make your life easier. They've *really* changed ours for the better.

The Communication Toolbox

1. **Avoid absolutes:** *Never say never.* When we use an "absolute" in communication, we leave no room for compromise, for difference of opinion, or for sharing of blame. Just the insertion of this one word can end an effective communication before it's even begun! Some absolutes that we may grab for every day include *always, never, all the time, only, everybody, every time, impossible, none, forever, totally,* and so on. For example: "You *never* call when you say you're going to," or "*Everyone* else is going!" or "You *always* roll your eyes when I say that." Watch what happens when you swap in an *often*, or a *sometimes*. Magic.

2. **Add some "I" statements:** An "I" statement is most easily formed by adding an "I feel like ___" to the opening of the next heated one-liner you're about to spout (and perhaps regret later). For example, "*I feel like* you never call when you say you're going to ..." instantly allows for the personal reality; this is your opinion, not the absolute truth (however much we all know we're *always* right). We've found that this one little add-in makes it much less likely that the other person will be instantly insulted or put on the defensive before the real communication has even begun.

3. **Active listening:** We all know the basic signs of when we're actually being listened to: eye contact, body language that is focused toward you and not toward another task (like email or a text message); some regular verbal affirmations (like "Yeah" or "Mmm-hmm"); natural nodding of the head; and so on. Our communications are more effective when we feel that we are being actively listened to rather than being sort of halfway listened to, and when we are actively listening in return rather than passively zoning out or simply preparing our next *brilliant* comeback. The fact is, you're not going to *get it* unless you

really listen, and you're not going to be *gotten unless she's* really listening. It's the team approach to effective communication.

4. **The three layers of communication:** The three layers are (1) what you said, (2) how you said it, and (3) the face you made when saying it. We often focus on the *content* of our communications—the actual words we use ("I can't believe she said *that!*"). But more often than not it is our tone or body language that sends the real message and throws an effective communication off the tracks. There are some amazing studies that show that body language and tone often communicate *tons* more than our actual words. In fact, 55 percent of our feelings are communicated by our facial expressions and body language, 38 percent of our feelings are communicated by our tone and manner of speaking, and only 7 percent of our feelings are communicated by our actual words.[7] Yes! Believe it! It can be confusing, frustrating, and even painful when we receive communications that send contradictory messages. For example, your friend might say she is sorry, but you don't feel like she means it (you could tell by the tone she uses and the way she smiles). Or another friend says she's not mad at you, but her crossed arms and curt answers tell a different story. Take a look at your own habits and communication patterns and try to get your three different "layers" aligned so that you're not sending mixed messages. And when you feel like you're getting a mixed message, call out that person—kindly, please. For example, "You say you're happy, but you really don't look it. What's up?"

5. **Speak the truth:** In Eliza's opinion, the biggest and best gift that daughters can give their moms is frequent, honest, and no-attitude-filled communication. We've often found that girls are afraid of hurting their moms' feelings with their honesty. Remember that your mom is an adult—and if you can be courageously kind *and* honest, well then, you have nothing to fear! Sil would like to add that moms need to make it safe to do so and

lead by honest and authentic example. Easier said than done, we know, but honesty does come with huge rewards. We promise.

PREPARING FOR APPRECIATION AND FEEDBACK

Daughtering To-Do: Get a journal or notebook and a pen, and spend ten to fifteen minutes making a list of things that your mom does that you *love*. Begin with the phrase: "Mom, I love it when you ____" and fill in the blank for yourself. These are what we call *appreciation communications,* and it's your job to come up with at least three. Write down a specific, and perhaps recent, example of a situation in which each one of these things has occurred.

Next, spend ten to fifteen minutes making a list of things that your mom does that you don't like so much. Begin with the phrase: "Mom, I really wish you wouldn't ____" and fill in the blank for yourself. These are *feedback communications.* Again, come up with three. Write down a specific, and perhaps recent, example of a situation in which one of these not-so-pleasant things happened.

Taking into account that your mom is a full, imperfect human being, is there a way the situation could have been different? See if you can avoid listing *character traits* that frustrate you (like you wish your mom didn't have such an "obnoxious" laugh, which she probably can't change), and focus instead on *behaviors* that she *could* change (for example, you wish she wouldn't talk to all of your aunts about your personal secrets, latest body developments, and love interests). Write honestly and from the heart. All of your lists are *private.* There is nothing you *have* to share.

Mothering To-Do: As your daughter writes, go back and reread chapter 4, "Mirroring a Soul." This will help you remember that your job is to really *get* what your daughter is saying—to actively listen, to mirror, and to contain. This kind of deep, personal conversation may be new for your daughter, as she may feel she is taking a big risk telling you things she has been afraid to tell you. Meet her with openness, and make your best effort to welcome both her appreciation and her feedback, however challenging it may be. Remember not to take her feedback personally. Throughout the exercise, you must be the adult watching out for your own preexisting assumptions, triggers, and negative patterns or ruts that tend to get you stuck in nonproductive interactions. Your goal is to be present and to genuinely hear your daughter—not to be a doormat to her feedback! Remember, your confident presence will help her brave young soul emerge.

Mothering Guidance

Use this CALM technique to help you remember how you want to be during conversations with your daughter:[8]

- **C:** Connect and make eye contact.
- **A:** Match the Affect of your daughter.
- **L:** Listen to what she is saying.
- **M:** Mirror and reflect back to show true understanding.

Ready to move on? Take a second to regroup, put aside your pencils and paper, and read our sample communications. These are real conversations—one for appreciation and one for feedback—that we have had (more than once) about simple things in our everyday lives.

An Appreciation Conversation

Eliza: Hey, Mom, I've got something I want to tell you.
Sil: I'm all ears.
Eliza: Well, you know how every morning when I get up at 7:30 for school, and I rush out the door forty-five minutes later only half-awake, and I'm always running late, but you are usually so energetic. You compliment me, or say something really nice

and encouraging, like, "Honey, you look so beautiful today." Or, "Good luck with your track meet! You're gonna rock it!"

Sil: Uh-huh?

Eliza: Well, I really like it that you do that.

Sil: Oh good, I'm glad it helps. I love being up with you in the morning.

Eliza: Yeah. You have to say that; you're my mom.

Sil: Not at all. I say it because I mean it.

Eliza: Sometimes I feel badly that I'm so rushed and grumpy. That I don't return the favor or at least acknowledge how nice it is what you said.

Sil: Mmm. I don't experience you as grumpy as much as tired and quiet. I don't mind the silence.

Eliza: Okay, well never mind that. But listen—this is what I wanted to say: I know I almost always shrug your compliments off, or roll my eyes or get frustrated, but honestly I really appreciate how you are with me in the mornings. It kind of starts my day off right. I guess if you didn't do it, I would miss it. So what I'm trying to say is, please don't stop.

Sil: I'm glad to know it matters to you. Thank you so much for telling me.

Eliza: Not a prob. But listen—it doesn't mean I'm going to be any better at receiving compliments at 7:30 a.m. It's really early in the morning. I'll try, though.

Sil: It *is* early in the morning. And I appreciate that you'll try.

A Feedback Conversation

Eliza: Hey, Mom, I've got something I want to talk to you about.

Sil: Okay. Just let me finish this one email—last sentence . . . Okay, ready! Shoot!

Eliza: I just get really frustrated when you say you're listening, but I know you're not. Like every evening when you say you're there, and you want to hear about my day, but you're always on the phone or answering a work email or taking care of someone else! You say I'm the one that's gone, that I shut you out now, but you don't seem to realize that you're *never* there!

Sil: Wow. I must be pretty blind to this—I didn't realize I do this so much. I am kind of shocked.

Eliza: Never mind. Forget I said anything. It doesn't matter.

Sil: No, no, no! I'm so glad you're telling me. I'm human, so it's a little challenging to hear about the ways I need to change. But I don't want you to hold it in, and most of all, I don't want to be distracted when we're together.

Eliza: Okay. So . . .

Sil: So tell me if I have it right. What you're saying is that I'm always distracted by something else—that I'm never fully there, even when I say I'm there?

Eliza: Like whenever I want to talk to you about something, there's just never a free moment. There's always somebody else or a work call or something.

Sil: Yeah, wow, that must be really frustrating for you.

Eliza: It *is*. And then you accuse me of shutting you out and hiding in my room or not telling you anything, but I feel like you're not there either!

Sil: I mean, I'm talking to you now. I'm here now.

Eliza: Yeah, well this is really unusual. It's like a miracle or something. Hallelujah.

Sil: Wait, wait, wait. Is it really this black and white, or is it more shades of gray? I know I give you my full attention some of the time, and you're also right, a lot of the time, even without realizing it, I'm busy with everything else in my life: work, our family, and just organizing the logistics of our lives, but not really dealing with the real stuff—the heart stuff, what's most important.

Eliza: I guess. Whatever. I guess I *feeeeel* like you're never there.

Sil: Thanks, that makes a big difference, and yeah, that feeling must be really hard. I *want* to be there for you, and I'm so sorry you don't feel like I am. Why don't we figure out how I can be? I want to do it differently. I want to get better at this.

Eliza: I don't know. Maybe you could stop doing email when I'm home in the evenings.

Sil: Well, sometimes I do have to send a few emails, but maybe we could plan it so that I write them while you're doing your homework? Like when you feel like you need to go into your room for some personal space, I could do work then.

Eliza: Okay, that makes sense.

Sil: But if we're both just sitting in the same room, will you actually talk to me? You always get so frustrated when I ask you about your day.

Eliza: I don't know. Maybe. Ask me a more specific question and maybe I'll answer it. I hate that general "How was your day?" My day was lots of *different* ways.

Sil: Okay. I can do that. And I can really pay attention to actually paying attention to you when we're talking. To not being distracted.

Eliza: Thanks. I would like that.

Sil: And thank you for bringing this up. I'm glad you did.

Eliza: Yup. Me too, I guess.

When a conversation gets heated, you may need a different CALM technique:[9]

C: Cool down. Self-soothe and control yourself, but without trying to control your daughter.

A: Assess options. What are the issues? Would it be better to keep talking or to postpone until you both have cooled down and connected?

L: Listen with empathy and without buts. And if you get agitated again, start over.

M: Make a plan. Consider ways to handle the meltdown and move forward.

The Appreciation and Feedback Exercise

1. Sit down facing each other on the same level and in such a way that your eyes naturally meet each other's. Make sure you have extra cushions so you're totally comfortable.

2. Pause and take a moment to check in with yourself silently. How are you feeling? Find the most open and nonjudgmental place in yourself and tap into it, knowing that when we act from that most unguarded place, we have our most effective communications. Review the communication guidelines again: be aware of your absolutes ("always, never"), your body language, and your tone and volume. Remember to practice active listening (true presence) and to phrase your personal beliefs, feelings, and experiences in the form of "I" statements.

3. The daughter will open each communication with the simple phrase: "Hey, Mom, I've got something I want to talk to you about." Let this sentence become ritual; it can help you slip into a conversation that may otherwise feel difficult to start. (It may sound weird to you to have a ritual opening to some of your conversations, but try it. It works a lot better than you might think.) The daughter will then communicate a situation, feeling, or thought that has been on her mind lately. The mother's task is, first of all, simply to *get it*. Listen. The mother then mirrors her daughter's communication back, making sure, by asking for her daughter's confirmation, that she has indeed understood the point. If necessary, problem solving follows, with resolution as the final stage (which isn't necessarily a perfect agreement, but may be a compromise). See our conversations above for two example flows of communication. Consider making your first communication an appreciation conversation. Since appreciation conversations are almost always easier, it makes sense to start there, right? But if you're just *burning* to do a feedback

conversation, if you can't even *think* about doing an appreciation conversation until you've gotten something off your chest, then do that. Do whatever feels right to you. Go ahead. Dive in. "Mom, I've got something I want to talk to you about." It can be quite simple. *Go!* (Yes, we mean right now.) There. That wasn't so hard, was it? Good.

4. Now it's time for a feedback communication. Consider doing a "mock" conversation first, by either reading our feedback conversation above out loud as if it were your real situation or by using a "fake" communication that you know is a real situation for a close friend of yours. Doing either one of these things can lower the stakes. Then dive into the real stuff! Remember, there must be some kind of resolution point at the end of every communication.

5. Debriefing: How did it go? Were there certain places where you got stuck? Were there certain types of statements or comments that ticked you off or seemed to push all of your buttons? Were there other places where your conversation flowed easily? What do each of you want to work on? Is there anything you would like to agree to change? Pick at least one new thing you would like to commit to changing in the way you communicate with each other. (You don't have to follow every appreciation or feedback conversation in normal life with a debriefing. But as you work at first to get the hang of talking this way, it's a good idea.)

6. Do as many exercises as you want, need, and have time for!

Naming Your Treasure

What is your favorite thing about your relationship? What is it that makes *your* relationship unique? When do you have the most fun together? What do you really connect over? All of these questions lead to the same place: what you *treasure* the most in your relationship. Fundamentally, we believe that there is one main treasure—your relationship. But we'd like you to begin to identify the specific things that you treasure within your relationship, the things that you treasure within the treasure.

Exercise: Name Your Treasure

Take five minutes to each write in your journals about what is special to you about your relationship. What do you love? List at least three treasures. Share and compare.

Certain treasures may be found every day (like you have the same sense of humor). Other treasures may feel like they are becoming more and more rare (like having downtime or time together to do projects, go shopping, or just go for a walk with the dog). Now that you've identified your treasure(s) and have them all written down in a nice little list (this is key!), let's get real: *How* are you actually going to protect them from disappearing under the demands of daily life? In the face of overactive schedules, work, and family commitments, how can you safeguard them? How can you *both* stay true to your intention to keep your bond strong?

Exercise: Protect Your Treasure

What actions can you both commit to in order to keep the bond of your relationship, though always in transition, fundamentally strong? What would be fun? And, above all, what would actually work? Pause now and decide on at least one action. One, that's all! Be specific—exactly *what* will you do, *when, how frequently,* and *for how long?* How will you make sure that this activity is for just the two of you and not other family members? (Yes, of course, you love them too, but this particular thing is for *you*.) Is there another sibling who sometimes gets in the way of your unique relationship? Is your family split between more than one house? How do you create special time for *your* bond?

Pause and compare your daily schedules. When is there a time in your day when you could both commit to being together? *Really* being together, even if it's only for five minutes. Sometimes quality over quantity is the way to go. Really think about this. Be realistic. If you're not always in the same house every night, can you talk on the phone? In addition to your daily check-in, you'll also want to have one time a week—perhaps on the weekend—when you have at least an hour together, cooking, working on a project, or taking a walk. Your treasure needs this time: just one hour a week!

One mother-daughter pair we know does the three-word check-in every night before bed, and they've added their own personal touch to it: they each list three things that they are grateful for that day and share a little bit about each thing. Another mother-daughter pair we know checks in at the dinner table by sharing their emotional highs and lows for the day, or what they call their "roses and thorns." One good thing, one not-so-good thing—and this opens up the window into what their days have really been like. One of our all-time favorite ideas is a mother-daughter pair who protects the treasure of their relationship with regular back-and-forth writing in a shared journal. They take turns writing, and then they sneak the journal under each other's pillow. As one or the other gets into bed, surprise! This can be a neat and private way to keep talking if your schedules don't always line up. Also, some topics may be easier to talk about in writing than face-to-face. Some questions are just plain awkward! And some conversations you may never seem to have the right private moment for. Even if you don't have a lot of time, short entries that catch each other up and end with an XO can really make your day. The entries don't have to happen every day; find a rhythm that works for the two of you.

As we close our chapter and our book, let's remember the pages behind us. Daughters, we've traveled from intuition to paradox, from first periods to grandmothers, from red tents to emotional intelligence, from "ideal" beauty to redefining "fat," from feeling trusted to being the genuine you, and from wild mood swings to daughtering.

Mothers, we've traveled from instinct to attachment, from intuition to brain science, from mirroring to passing on a healthy body image, from containing to community, from matrilineal inheritance to matrilineal healing, and from Demeter's determination to slow mothering.

And now we find ourselves here, at the close, learning to communicate better with each other and making a plan to protect the treasure that is our relationship.

Getting along is work, hard work. There will always be ruptures—both big and small; but there will also *always, always* be the potential for repair. The world we live in today does not make *real* mother-daughter relationships an easy thing. We are told, and you will likely hear a hundred times in the years to come, that mothers and teen daughters *do not get along*. We, however (yes, all four of us), know differently, and we challenge you two to prove the world wrong, to show them the real truth and heart of the matter.

What you have in your hands is a toolbox—one that is built to help you find and protect the treasure of your unique relationship. It is unique because no one, anywhere, connects just like you. There is no "perfect" mother, and there is no "perfect" daughter, but there *is* authenticity, humor, truth, trust, and love. Let them be your goals instead.

Notes

1. Alexander Afanasev, Maria Tatar, ed., "Vasilisa the Fair," *The Annotated Classic Fairy Tales* (New York: W. W. Norton, 2002).

2. Marion Woodman and Robert Bly, *The Maiden King: The Reunion of Masculine and Feminine* (New York: Holt Paperbacks, 1999).

3. Elizabeth Lesser, *Broken Open: How Difficult Times Can Help Us Grow* (New York: Villard, 2005).

4. Rachel Kauder Nalebuff, ed., *My Little Red Book* (New York: Twelve, 2009), 1.

5. Courtney E. Martin, *Perfect Girls, Starving Daughters: How the Quest for Perfection Is Harming Young Women* (New York: Free Press, 2007).

6. Geneen Roth, *Women Food and God* (New York: Scribner, 2010), 211.

7. Albert Mehrabian, *Silent Message: Implicit Communication of Emotions and Attitudes* (New York: Wadsworth Publishing Company, 1972).

8. Jennifer Colari, *Connected Parenting: Transform Your Challenging Child and Build Loving Bonds for Life* (New York: Avery, 2009), 27.

9. Laura S. Kastner and Jennifer Wyatt, *Getting to Calm: Cool-headed Strategies for Parenting Tweens and Teens* (Seattle: Parent Map, 2009), 43.

*An ongoing list of daughtering resources and Eliza's fave "girl guides" is available online at motheringanddaughtering.com/daughteringresources. Check it out!